DOING WHAT WE CAME TO DO

DOING WHAT
WE CAME TO DO

living a life of love

ARDETH G. KAPP

DESERET
BOOK ®

Salt Lake City, Utah

Library of Congress Cataloging-in-Publication Data
Kapp, Ardeth G. (Ardeth Greene), author.
    Doing what we came to do : living a life of love / Ardeth G. Kapp.
        pages   cm
    Includes bibliographical references.
    ISBN 978-1-60908-743-2 (hardbound : alk. paper)
    1. Christian life—Mormon authors.   2. Love—Religious aspects—
Church of Jesus Christ of Latter-day Saints.   3. Church of Jesus Christ
of Latter-day Saints—Doctrines.   I. Title.
    BX8656.K365 2012
    248.4'88332—dc23   2011046521

Printed in the United States of America
Malloy Lithographing Incorporated, Ann Arbor, MI

10   9   8   7   6   5   4   3   2   1

contents

Contents

Keeping in Touch

Principles and Promises

God's Love

PREFACE

$\mathcal{A}$ song that became popular in the late 1940s teaches a wonderful truth: "Love is where you find it, don't be blind, it's all around you everywhere." But sadly, we live in a time when people are often isolated and hungry for a feeling of love and acceptance. In today's troubled world, the forces of evil are also all around us everywhere, attacking on every front. The enemy is real and is using every tactic possible to stir up emotions far removed from feelings of love.

Love is an attribute that we each have within us. It is not something we gain but rather something we develop. As President George Q. Cannon taught, "We are the children of God, and as his children there is no attribute we ascribe to Him that we do not possess, though they maybe dormant or in embryo" (*Gospel Truth,* 3).

The healing influence of love becomes a blessing to the one who gives and the one who receives. The power of love gives meaning and purpose to life. Love reaches beyond the borders of our challenges, and we find ourselves doing what we came to earth to do. At the close of the Savior's mortal ministry, in His last far-reaching message to His Apostles, He instructed, "A new commandment I give unto you, That ye love one another; as I have loved you, that ye also love one another" (John 13:34).

President Thomas S. Monson tells us, "Love is the catalyst that causes change. Love is the balm that brings healing to the soul. But love doesn't grow like weeds or fall like rain. Love has its price. 'God so loved the world, that he gave his only begotten Son, that whosoever believeth in him should not perish, but have everlasting life' (John 3:16). The Son, even the Lord Jesus Christ, gave His life that we might have eternal life, so great was His love for His Father and for us" ("The Doorway of Love," 2).

With sincere feelings of love in my heart for you, I share these chapters with a desire that the message will increase your awareness of the powerful gift of love. I pray you will feel that power whenever you are prompted by the Spirit to say a word, do a deed, think a thought, send a note, or say a prayer, acknowledging that you care.

In the words of the Prophet Joseph Smith, "When

persons manifest the least kindness and love to me, O what power it has over my mind, while the opposite course has a tendency to harrow up all the harsh feelings and depress the human mind" (*Teachings: Joseph Smith,* 428).

Living a life of love helps fill the measure of our creation. It's doing what we came to do.

IT IS
WITHIN YOU

Chapter 1

LOOK INSIDE YOURSELF

I once asked a young girl who was visiting me, "Are you the smartest one in your fourth-grade class?" She quickly responded in a positive tone, "No, I'm second smartest, but Jimmy is the last smartest." There was no question in her young mind where she stood.

I suppose each one of us has had experiences when we have felt like the second smartest. And we've probably also had times when we've felt like we were the last smartest. This affects our confidence and our ability to show love. The adversary would, if possible, have us believe we are way below average. But maybe it really doesn't matter if we are the last smartest, whether in the fourth-grade class or in any other category. Maybe the things that matter come from deeper within.

In the novel *The Chosen,* by Chaim Potok, the Jewish father cries out to the Master of the Universe in behalf of his son, who has a brilliant and capable mind. The father says, "A mind like this I need for a son? A *heart* I need for a son, a *soul* I need for a son, *compassion* I want from my son, righteousness, mercy, strength to suffer and carry pain, *that* I want from my son, not a mind without a soul!" (264; emphasis in original). Speaking of his own father, he says, "He taught me to look inside myself, to find my own strength, to walk around inside myself in company with my soul" (265). I imagine that his father probably said to him, "Son, it is within you. Look inside."

At times we each may ponder the question, "Is it within me?" Our Father invites us to ask ourselves this and then listen to the whisperings of the Spirit for a confirmation. The Lord said, "Behold, the kingdom of God is within you" (Luke 17:21), and "Ye shall seek me, and find me, when ye shall search for me with all your heart" (Jeremiah 29:13).

But there is a storm at sea. It's no ordinary storm. The world is in chaos. Dark clouds can dim our view of all that is important, causing us to doubt our abilities and question our resolve. Many are being tossed to and fro for want of an ethical compass.

The hymn "Jesus, Savior, Pilot Me" (*Hymns,* no. 104) offers the following insight:

Jesus, Savior, pilot me
Over life's tempestuous sea;
Unknown waves before me roll,
Hiding rock and treach'rous shoal.
Chart and compass came from thee;
Jesus, Savior, pilot me.

Yes, the chart and compass come from Him. In times of turbulence, we can be assured that the Master who calmed the storms on the Sea of Galilee can calm the storms in our personal and individual lives because He knows us and He knows the storm. He tells us, "Look unto me in every thought, doubt not, fear not" (Doctrine and Covenants 6:36).

Years ago Elder Oscar A. Kirkham, a great Church leader, spoke of three principles that have been like anchors for me. He simply said, "Build a sea-worthy ship, be a loyal shipmate, and sail a true course."

When the storms are at their peak in your life and the wind is blowing, is your ship seaworthy? Will you be a loyal shipmate, even when others may be abandoning ship and going in a direction that appears appealing, enticing, inviting, and, by the world's standards, glamorous? Is it within you to set sail against the wind and follow a true course?

The words of Job provide a measurement for our commitment to our highest priorities. At the very height of his seemingly unreasonable, unexplainable, unfair tests, he declared, "Till I die I will not remove mine integrity from me" (Job 27:5).

Integrity is the key to sailing a true course. If we have integrity, we will make our actions consistent with our knowledge of right and wrong. By contrast, if we know one thing and do another, our behavior creates an inner conflict and makes it impossible to feel at peace. We simply cannot think one way and act another. We must have integrity if we are to have peace within and feel God's love.

I would like to suggest three Ps that are essential to finding peace within: Ponder, Pray, and Prune. These can become life savers in turbulent storms.

Ponder

It is impossible to measure the benefits of thoughtful pondering, meditating, and listening—away from the turbulence of the world—where the Spirit can speak to us and where we can listen and hear.

Consider the experience of Nephi when he said, "I sat pondering" (1 Nephi 11:1). How long has it been since you've sat pondering, when the TV wasn't on and you weren't monitoring your cell phone? Is there ever a time like that? There was a time when Nephi sat pondering, and as he did, the Spirit said unto him, "What desirest thou?" (1 Nephi

11:2). And he knew what he desired. He was ready to answer.

Now, if the Spirit said to you or me, "What desirest thou?" would we have a long inventory of a hundred things we want? Of course we would. We're mortal, we're normal, and yes, we have a lot of desires.

But when we sit thoughtfully pondering in a quiet place and the Spirit speaks to us, there will come into our hearts and souls the things that are truly our greatest desires, those things that are more important in the long run than anything else. Away from the appeal of the world, that greatest desire usually relates to relationships with family and with the Lord. And when that priority is in place, then we begin to plan our lives with purpose. We begin to have goals that cause us to live with anticipation.

When we take time to thoughtfully ponder, we will be filled with the Spirit within. We know what we are working for and living for. We know what we want to have happen. Then, with each large or small decision we make, we draw upon the greatest of all blessings—that of personal revelation and agency. We ask ourselves, "Will this decision move me toward or away from my deepest desire, my ultimate goal?" This question is a protection against giving up what we want most for what we want now. It helps ensure that lifetime goals are never sacrificed for instant gratification.

Pray

From a lifetime of experience, I can tell you of the sure knowledge I have of the power of prayer. We have a direct line of communication with our Father in Heaven. When we get up in the morning, we can kneel in prayer and ask for the Spirit of God to be with us all day. At night, before we end the day, we can review our actions of the day and give thanks for any direction given by the promptings of the Spirit. We can ask forgiveness for the times when we may have not measured up. We are able to repent and ask for help every day.

President Boyd K. Packer said, "If you need a transfusion of spiritual strength, then just ask for it. We call that prayer. Prayer is powerful spiritual medicine" ("Balm of Gilead," 18). Is it any wonder that we're warned that we must "watch and pray always lest [we] enter into temptation; for Satan desireth to have [us], that he may sift [us] as wheat" (3 Nephi 18:18).

How important is prayer? In a revelation given to the Prophet Joseph Smith, the Lord counseled, "Pray always lest that wicked one have power in you, and remove you out of your place" (Doctrine and Covenants 93:49).

We ponder, we pray, and then, directed by the Spirit, we prune.

Prune

The adversary would, if possible, like to keep us busily engaged in a multitude of things—even *good* things—that would distract us from the few things that make all the difference. Pruning may require cutting back, eliminating, and discarding distractions. These may not necessarily be bad things. More likely, we will find that it is some of the nonessential distractions that can weigh us down. Like the early pioneers, who had to decide what they would make room for in their wagons and what they were willing to leave behind in order to reach their destination, we have decisions to make that may not be easy. Regardless of the standards of the world, the early pioneers had to make choices according to what they knew was essential to realize their most earnest desires. Pruning takes careful thought concerning what we really want to have happen after all is said and done.

Ponder. Pray. Prune. You have it within you to be a true disciple of Jesus Christ, not perfect yet, but on the way. You have it within your heart and soul. Can you feel it now? Do you know in your heart, through the witness of the Spirit, that it is within you to be everything that you've been destined to be? Keep that fire burning.

Chapter 2

THE LIGHT WITHIN

A few years ago I met a remarkable young woman who radiates the light of Christ with a glow that illuminates her circle of influence in an inspiring way. Her name is Annae Jensen Jones. She and her husband came to the Cardston Alberta Temple when my husband and I were serving there. Annae was blessed with eyes to see and ears to hear and thoughts to ponder and earnest desires to pursue and a heart to love. Annae had developed a remarkable gift of love, both to receive it and to give it. She had many blessings, but not all. She was born without arms. Because prosthetic limbs do not work for her, she uses her feet for everything she does—and she does everything.

I have a video showing Annae as a child learning to ride a bicycle, using her shoulders on the extended handlebars, falling down and getting up, falling down and getting up. With the power of love, her wise parents permitted and even encouraged the difficult process until she mastered it. Later she learned to drive a car with her feet on the steering wheel. She blow dries her hair and applies makeup, does the cooking, and on and on with incredible determination and skill.

Can you picture this young mother cradling her precious new baby—not in her arms but with her legs and feet, sitting down? "Happiness is an attitude," Annae says with a winning smile. "I can be happy and deal with it or I can be unhappy about it and end up not reaching my potential." Following a women's conference in Calgary, Alberta, I was able to hold her precious baby in my arms, and I marveled at the radiant spirit of this young mother filled with light and love. I wished there could be some arrangement whereby I could literally give her my arms to hold her baby for a little while, and then she could let me be the mother and hold her baby in my arms.

Annae has two children. She explained that when her little two-year-old wants to be picked up, the child has to hold on. Is that not a message for each of us? If we want to be lifted up, we must "hold on."

Annae's example shows us that when we magnify the abilities we do have, we are able to compensate for what we don't have at this time. We focus our attention on our potential rather than our limitations. We see things from a different perspective.

The great Christian writer C. S. Lewis gives us this thought: "The real problem of the Christian life comes where people do not usually look for it. It comes the very moment you wake up each morning. All your wishes and hopes for the day rush at you like wild animals. And the first job each morning consists simply in shoving them all back; in listening to that other voice, taking that other point of view, letting that other larger, stronger, quieter life come flowing in. And so on, all day. Standing back from all your natural fussings and frettings; coming in out of the wind. We can only do it for moments at first. But from those moments the new sort of life will be spreading through our system: because now we are letting Him work at the right part of us. It is the difference between paint, which is merely laid on the surface, and a dye or stain which soaks right through. . . . When He said, 'Be perfect,' He meant it. He meant that we must go in for the full treatment" (*Mere Christianity*, 198).

I believe Annae and her husband, Gareth, are in for the full treatment—not just a "paint," but a "stain which soaks right through."

What was it that fueled the fire of commitment, determination, endurance, and unwavering faith in those early pioneers who came before us? How were they able to carry on through such adversity and persecution? Those pioneers were driven by a cause greater than themselves. They had an eternal perspective and an understanding that others were counting on them.

The tender, revealing words of Vilate Chamberlain Raile, one of those early pioneers, offers a glimpse of that perspective:

> *They cut desire into short lengths*
> *And fed it to the hungry fire of courage.*
> *Long after—when the flames died—*
> *Molten gold gleamed in the ashes.*
> *They gathered it into bruised palms*
> *And handed it to their children*
> *And their children's children.*
>
> (As quoted in *Selected Writings of Gerald N. Lund,* 402–3)

I ponder the words of my great-great-grandmother Sarah Sturdevant Leavitt, another early pioneer, whose husband died before they reached the valley. She traveled on with her young family to the valley of the Great Salt Lake. In her journal we read these words, which tell something of what she felt in her heart:

"To write my love of God above it would drain the ocean, though the sea was ink, and the earth paper and every stick a pen and every man a scribe. When I try to praise Him in beauty, to honor and magnify the name of God, I find I have no language at my command that will do justice to the case, but when I lay aside this weak, frail body I expect to praise Him in the beauty of holiness."

Our Father gives us a vision of His glorious work, His love for us, and our grand possibilities, even in the face of trials and adversity. "For behold, this is my work and my glory—to bring to pass the immortality and eternal life of man" (Moses 1:39).

a Feeling of Worth

Feeling loved, with an assurance of our infinite worth, has a tremendous effect on our ability to accept and love others. To feel loved is to feel valued, accepted, and appreciated for who we "really" are and for who we are capable of becoming. In the words of Elder Jeffrey R. Holland: "God doesn't care nearly as much about where you have been as he does about where you are, and with his help where you are willing to go" ("Remember Lot's Wife," n. p.).

This feeling of self-worth comes from an inner sense of our true eternal identity as a son or daughter of God. Self-worth cannot be earned. It is a part of our divine nature as children of God. Looking inside ourselves with an eternal perspective of our divine heritage and infinite worth allows us to be more receptive to expressions of love and to express love.

The source of all righteous love is centered in God. A feeling of self-worth comes from an understanding of who we were, who we are, and who we will always be. We did not come to this earth to gain our worth; we brought it with us.

Throughout the scriptures the Lord emphasizes the worth of a person as "precious" (Psalm 49:8; Alma 31:35), "great" (Doctrine and Covenants 18:10), and "more precious than fine gold" (Isaiah 13:12). Self-worth cannot be increased or decreased. The worth of every soul that has ever lived is absolute and infinite. It is the same for everyone. No matter what our circumstances or appearance or social status, we have worth as God's creation!

There is a difference between self-esteem and self-worth. Self-esteem is defined as "a confidence and satisfaction in oneself" (*Merriam-Webster's Collegiate Dictionary,* s.v. "self-esteem"). In other words, it's *your* perspective of yourself. "Self-esteem is the glue that holds together our self-reliance, our self-control, our self-approval, and keeps all self-defense mechanisms secure" (James E. Faust, "Self-Esteem: A Great Human Need," 191).

Self-esteem can be positive or negative. For example, we talk about a person having low or negative self-esteem. We all know people who lack confidence, who often speak critically of themselves. Circumstances of life appear to have a tremendous influence on self-esteem, to the extent that people who have been verbally, emotionally, or physically abused may even respond as they have been treated. In the movie *My Fair Lady,* Eliza Doolittle tells Henry Higgins, "The difference between a lady and a flower girl is not how she behaves, but how she is treated." That's a challenge we all face—to not allow our perception of ourselves to be negatively impacted by the way we might sometimes be treated.

On the other hand, self-worth cannot be earned or affected by anything that may happen in this life. Worth is constant and unchanging. It is a fact that worthiness does not determine worth. You cannot sin enough to change your worth to the Lord who loves you. In Jacob 2:21 this principle is explained very clearly: "And the one being is as precious in his sight as the other."

When we experience a feeling of God's view of our worth, we are better able to feel His unconditional love for us, to remember who we really are, and to believe we are who God says we are—a son or daughter of God with a divine inheritance.

Elder Boyd K. Packer points out the importance of recognizing one's self-worth in light of the difficulties we experience in the world today. He said, "No idea has been more *destructive* of happiness, no philosophy has produced more sorrow, more heartbreak and mischief; no idea has done more to destroy the family than the idea that we are not the offspring of God" ("Our Moral Environment," 67; emphasis in original). In addition,

Elder Robert C. Oaks reminds us of the dire consequences of "the theft of our eternal identity." He explains, "I am not talking about addresses, credit cards, or any other identifying numbers. I am talking about something much more basic and more important than who the world thinks you are. I am talking about who *you* think you are. . . . Satan is totally dedicated to thwarting and derailing this marvelous plan-of-happiness knowledge and process. We know that one of his primary tools is to entice us to forget who we really are—to fail to realize or to forget our divine potential. This is the cruelest form of identity theft" ("Your Divine Heritage," 49; emphasis in original).

I think we innocently allow the theft of our "identity" by focusing more on our esteem than on our worth. It is not until you and I comprehend the magnitude of our eternal destiny—who we are and Whose we are—and find peace, regardless of life's circumstances, that we reach our potential. Recognizing our self-worth controls ultimately our ability to love God, to love others, to love life, and to love ourselves.

The need to feel loved is basic to our ability to love one another and to believe in every person's divine nature and individual worth. This inner assurance releases a powerful force for good. When we strive to see each other as our Father sees us, we will look not on the outward appearance and imperfections of a brother or sister or ourselves, not on the person that we are, but on the angel we may become.

Chapter 4

FULL OF JOY

he scriptures tell us, "Men are, that they might have joy" (2 Nephi 2:25). And we are told that we shouted for joy in anticipation of our time here on earth with its purpose and plan.

Our time is our life, and however we use our time, we pay for those choices with our life. That is a rather sobering but also exciting thought to contemplate. Life is a precious gift. What have you done today worth paying for with your life?

Some time ago I was invited to a birthday dinner for Sister Norma Alder. She was a widow living alone, had just turned 100 years of age, and was almost totally blind. Over the years she had experienced the realities of mortality and the challenges that are an essential part of this life.

The conversation with Sister Alder was amazing, enlightening, and full of enthusiasm. She was very alert and fun to talk with. She reported that she had been a visiting teacher for seventy-seven years. She said that when she went out to weed her flower garden, she had to be very careful to pull the weeds and not the flowers; with her deteriorating eyesight, it wasn't easy to tell the difference. Her grandchildren teased her by telling her, "Grandma, act your age!"

I asked Sister Alder, "How do you stay so alert and informed?" Without hesitation she responded, "Well, when I have time I listen to tapes and the radio and try to keep up on things."

I thought, "When you have time? Is this matter of time still a challenge at 100 years of age?" Over the years she had obviously learned to pull the weeds and save the flowers.

Sometimes we unknowingly pull what would become flowers and leave the weeds. Or we find ourselves wishing we were in someone else's garden. Comparing, competing, and complaining leave us unsettled and dissatisfied.

I like to feast on the words of Ralph Waldo Emerson: "There is a time in every man's education when he arrives at the conviction that envy is ignorance, that imitation is suicide; that he must take himself for better or worse as his portion; that though the wide universe is full of good, no nourishing kernel of corn can come to him but through his toil bestowed upon that plot of ground given to him to till. The power which resides in him is new in nature, and none but he knows what that is that he can do, nor does he know until he has tried.

"What I must do is all that concerns me, not what the people think. This rule, equally arduous in actual and in intellectual life, may serve for the whole distinction between greatness and meanness. It is the harder, because you will always find those who think they know what is your duty better than you know it. It is easy in the world to live after the world's opinion; it is easy in solitude to live after your own, but the great man is he who in the midst of the crowd keeps with perfect sweetness the independence of solitude" ("Self-Reliance," 263).

In our busy lives, we may look but not see, we may listen but not hear, we may think but not ponder. We can see life in many different ways—with the eye, with the mind, but most importantly with the heart. We see what we are looking for, burdens or blessings, weeds or flowers. And sometimes we need help from the Gardener.

In words shared by Rachel Remeen, "Days pass and the years vanish and we walk sightless among miracles. Lord, fill our eyes with seeing and our minds with knowing. Let there be moments when your Presence, like lightning, illuminates the darkness in which we walk. Help us to see, wherever we gaze, that the bush burns, unconsumed. And we, clay touched by God, will reach out for holiness and exclaim in wonder, 'How filled with awe is this place and we did not know it'" (*My Grandfather's Blessings*, 72–73).

Elizabeth Barrett Browning said it another way:

Earth's crammed with heaven,
And every common bush afire with God:
But only he who sees takes off his shoes,
The rest sit round it, and pluck blackberries . . .

("Aurora Leigh," Book VII, lines 21–24)

Do we see the burning bush, or do the blackberries claim our attention? I believe there is a spiritual meaning to all earthly events, and when we view daily happenings with an eternal perspective, we are privileged not only to witness miracles but to participate in them. Like Sister Alder, may we weed and tend our plots of ground over the seasons of our lives in such a way as to reap a great harvest.

IT IS WITHIN you:
PONDER, ASK, ACT

Ponder

Think about your infinite worth, your divine nature, and your
unlimited possibilities.

Ask

Do I recognize the light within?
Am I looking in the right direction?
What are my most earnest desires?
Do I understand my true identity?
Am I spending my life on things that matter?
Am I enjoying the daily miracles of life?
What might I start doing or stop doing to make a positive
change?

Act

Remember the times you have felt success.
Prioritize your goals.
Pray for strength, for help in specific areas.
Keep your mind focused on positive things.
Remember your true identity as a son or daughter of God who
loves you.
Love one another.
Enjoy the journey.

you know
enough

Chapter 5

DIFFERENT BUT NOT DUMB

I have a book entitled *If You Are Not from the Prairie,* which lists all the things you don't know—can't know— if you're not from the prairie. Another book could be written about what you don't and can't know if you're not from the mountains or the city or if you're not from Oklahoma or Los Angeles or New York. Basically, anyone in the world could say, "If you have not walked in my shoes, you don't know what I know. You can't know what I know."

Although that is true, there *are* some important things common to all of us that we do know about each other, things that draw us together in a very significant way, regardless of age or circumstances, location or interests. When we understand our relationship as sisters, the bond of sisterhood can enrich our lives in a most remarkable way.

Learning to recognize people's gifts and talents, including our own, as a rich reservoir from which we might all draw provides a wealth of experiences.

It is essential to our mission as sisters in the gospel that we nurture the gifts given each one of us and also help nurture the gifts of others. "For all have not every gift given unto them; for there are many gifts, and to every man [and woman] is given a gift by the Spirit of God" (Doctrine and Covenants 46:11). The plan of the adversary would, if possible, have us compare, compete, and complain. He seeks to weaken our own confidence and even, by our careless gossip, diminish and demean the gifts of others.

Just recently I caught myself trying to avoid negative thoughts of my own making. I had been invited to a gathering where a group of sisters were displaying the results of several months of creative work with knitting needles. There were unique designs with various colors of yarn, resulting in beautiful articles of clothing for children. I don't knit. In that setting I might have felt dumb.

When the delicious, unusual dessert was served and everyone discussed the details of the recipe, I might have felt dumb because I'm not a gourmet cook.

When people frequently say to me, "Oh, Sister Kapp, I just love your music," I have to respond, "No, you don't love my music. I'm not Janice Kapp Perry. She is my husband's cousin." Considering my lack of musical ability, I might feel dumb.

At every age and stage, if we were to feel envious of the gifts others have that we don't possess, we could feel dumb. But we must not. That thinking is a tool of the adversary. It is not according to the plan. I take great comfort in the words of Elder Neil L. Andersen: "'You don't know everything, but you know enough'—enough to keep the commandments and to do what is right" ("You Know Enough," 13).

Years ago, when I was teaching the fourth-grade class at Oak Hills Elementary School, I sensed the need to help every child avoid the debilitating experience of focusing on others' gifts and not recognizing their own.

"I'm dumb," Marty would whisper half under her breath as I would bend down to help her with her work. It seemed that her attitude about herself was more of a problem than her actual lack of ability.

One back-to-school night, after all the other parents had left the room, Marty's father remained. In his hand he held a small card. Like all the other children, Marty had prepared a sample of her work for her parents. Hers was made of light blue construction paper trimmed artistically with delicate paper cuttings of the most intricate design. I watched her father as he carefully opened the card, read again the brief but sensitive message inside, and then spoke with compassion and love. "She may be different," he said, dropping his eyes to look again at the card, "but she isn't dumb," he added with a tone of assurance.

"Marty," he explained, "has missed a lot of school over the past years because of illness, and as a result, she hasn't done as well as her older brothers and sisters. She has it so strongly implanted in her mind that she often says she is dumb. It's true, she is different." Then, after pausing a moment to be assured he had my full attention, he continued, "But she isn't dumb."

When someone, especially a parent, has confidence in a child, and that confidence is expressed consistently, the child's ability seems almost magically commensurate with the expressed confidence. I thought of Marty's great advantage in having a father who knew she wasn't dumb. For Marty, it was her father who understood something of her great potential and was speaking in her behalf. I thought of the great blessing we each have in having our Father who knows our potential and our Savior who is an advocate for each one of us (see Doctrine and Covenants 45:3).

Returning to the classroom, I thought, *Yes Marty, I do understand. You are different, just like every other student in this classroom; but you, like they, are not dumb, and somehow, some way you must find that out. There must be some way.*

The next morning the day was off to a good start—that is, until Brent noticed an unusually long list of assignments on the chalkboard. Instead of just one page of arithmetic, there were two. The same with spelling and English. In addition to the regular assignments for Wednesday, there were assignments in dictionary skills that were usually delayed until Friday. Added to all of that was an assignment for one piece of original art.

Immediately the anxiety level was evident. To the students' many questions I responded, "Yes, you are expected to have all the assignments completed by the end of the day." Then, to establish some kind of control, I extended both hands with palms down as if to keep the lid on the boiling pot. "Quiet down and let me explain," I said.

They seemed willing to listen to any explanation for such seeming inconsideration, and so I began. "We need to discover the great resources that we have in our classroom, and how dependent we are on each other. We cannot all do the same things equally well, and even if we could, it might not be the best way." To make the point, I asked Tiffany, whose father was a hairdresser, if he had built their house. She said she didn't know who had built it, but she was sure it hadn't been her dad. Then I asked whose father was a builder, and Charity told about all the houses her dad had built. Before long, everyone had joined in the discussion, and together we discovered the need for every dad's service and how dependent we all are on each other.

With that discussion as a base, I suggested to the students that today we would take advantage of the resources in our classroom. Each one could go to whomever they wished to get their work done—but it had to be a good job and they had to do something in return. Again the questions came, but with much more enthusiasm this time.

"You mean it's okay if I get Dave to do my arithmetic?" asked Linda, and I nodded approval. Then Timmy, who seemed to be the least artistic, spoke loud enough for all to hear, "And is it okay if Marty does my artwork?" Again I nodded, looking out of the corner of my eye to see a surprised expression on Marty's face. "You're getting the idea," I said. "It's called a division of labor, and we will use the expertise of everyone."

Without any discussion, it seemed every child knew which five or six students were the most able in math and had lined up to arrange for those services; the same for each of the other subjects. The excitement came after the experts had completed their own assignments and then had only to copy the answers onto six or eight other papers for their friends. Instead of taking all day as they had supposed, by lunchtime almost everyone was reporting with great excitement that all of their work was completed.

The one assignment that was taking longer than all the rest was the piece of original art. It was not so easily copied as math, spelling, or English, but without any question it was the most rewarding, the most successful, and the most important work of the day. Marty had a line of several students standing around her desk waiting their turn for her to help each one assemble the pattern she had cut for a beautiful collage of colors, textures, and designs.

With a big smile Marty glanced up and, as if she could contain the joy of her discovery not a moment longer, blurted out, "I'm not dumb after all!"

I turned my head quickly and casually walked over to my desk to avoid having to make an explanation to some curious student about "Why have you got tears in your eyes, Mrs. Kapp?"

The following day began with a long explanation of why it wasn't all right to always do our work that way, since it took less time and was better work. A lot more time was spent talking about the many talents, gifts, and abilities that were represented in our class, and what a serious loss it would be if even one were missing. Yesterday's work had been put away and almost forgotten, except for the artwork, which was artistically arranged on the front bulletin board for everyone to enjoy.

Surely the greatest and most important lesson, not only for Marty but for every child in the class, had been the discovery that we are all different, but not dumb. It does not matter if we come from the prairie or the mountain, from Manhattan, New York, or Paradise, Utah. The fact is, regardless of your circumstances, "you don't know everything, but you know enough"—enough to keep the commandments and do what is right and share your gifts and talents with others.

Chapter 6

OUR ADVANTAGE IN THE WORLD TO COME

Perhaps you read in the newspapers about a young woman who made history as the first woman to graduate at the top of her class at Harvard Law School. A faithful Latter-day Saint, she was also the first student in a decade and a half to get straight A's all three years. What a tremendous advantage she will enjoy as she pursues her life mission! And it doesn't stop there. The scriptures tell us, "Whatever principle of intelligence we attain unto in this life, it will rise with us in the resurrection. And if a person gains more knowledge and intelligence in this life through his diligence and obedience than another, he will have so much the advantage in the world to come" (Doctrine and Covenants 130:18–19).

How encouraging that declaration must be to this young

woman. But is it equally inspiring to those of us who may not have graduated at the top, or even the middle, of our classes? Does it mean there is no hope for us to rise in the resurrection with straight A's?

At a very early age, I became preoccupied, even obsessed, with that passage from the Doctrine and Covenants. It was very obvious to me that if you were smart, learned quickly, got good grades, and rose to the top, you certainly had an advantage here—no question. What consumed my growing concern was that you would also have "so much the advantage in the world to come." *Where is the justice?* I thought. To my young mind, it seemed clear that if you were smarter, the Lord had made you that way, and so He must love you more. And the reverse would also hold true.

I remember asking my father in anguish, "If the glory of God is intelligence, and you are not smart, what will happen to you?" And my wise and learned father, who never graduated from high school but was self-taught and intelligent through diligent study and great faith, eased my concern when he explained, "My dear, if you are diligent in your studies and do your very best and are obedient to God's commandments, one day, when you enter the holy temple, the university of the Lord, you will be prepared in your mind and spirit to learn and know all you need to know to return to your Father in Heaven." It was faith in that promise that seemed to unlock my mind. It was study and faith working together, along with obedience.

But that was years ago, when spelling bees and times tables measured one's preparation for the future, at least for the next grade.

What of today, with its computers, word processors, satellites, iPods, iPads, Blackberries, and newfound truth? Will we keep up? Should we? What learning should we seek? I determined that it was better that I focus my attention on understanding the meaning of *intelligence* rather than being preoccupied with the concept of *advantage.*

It is this attention that lifts, elevates, inspires, edifies, and can transform the "last smartest" to the top of the class, if they so desire. The scripture states, "The glory of God is intelligence, or, in other words, light and truth" (Doctrine and Covenants 93:36). And what are light and truth? Where are they to be found? What is the curriculum? Where does one register for that course or class?

The Prophet Joseph Smith received in revelation the answer to those questions: "The word of the Lord is truth, and whatsoever is truth is light, and whatsoever is light is Spirit, even the Spirit of Jesus Christ" (Doctrine and Covenants 84:45).

Attaining intelligence, then, is much more than merely mastering facts and their applications, however useful they may be. It is a process of the heart as well as of the mind. It is striving to understand the spirit, even the character, of Jesus Christ. The character of Christ has been defined as "the sum total of his characteristics, his moral traits, the features of his mind and heart and soul . . . his quality, his temper, his disposition, the stamp of his genius, the notes of his spirit, and the form of his conduct" (Charles Edward Jefferson, *The Character of Jesus,* 4). Such an education is a mighty, daunting task. But the means for achieving it are available to all, regardless of their intellectual endowments. For all who truly seek, the Lord has provided a divine, personal tutor.

Through baptism of the water and of the Spirit, and by obedience to the commandments, we qualify for the gift of the Holy Ghost, the greatest teacher—a teacher of light and truth. Consider this remarkable companionship to enhance our learning. As Elder Parley P. Pratt wrote, "It quickens all the intellectual faculties, increases, enlarges, expands, and purifies all the natural passions and affections. . . . It inspires virtue, kindness, goodness, tenderness, gentleness, and charity. It develops beauty of person, form, and features. It tends to health, vigor, animation, and social feeling. It invigorates all the faculties of the physical and intellectual man. It strengthens and gives tone to the nerves. In short, it is, as it were, marrow to the bone, joy to the heart, light to the eyes, music to the ears, and life to the whole being. . . . Such is the gift of the Holy Ghost, and such are its operations when received through the lawful channel—the divine, eternal priesthood" (*Key to the Science of Theology,* 61–62).

Our education is more than knowledge of facts and information, as important as that is. We have been instructed, "Seek ye out of the best books words of wisdom, seek learning even by study and also by faith" (Doctrine and Covenants 109:7). Our souls, body and spirit, should be filled with a desire to know the will of God, which is truth and light, and to become like Him. When that is our focus, our scholastic degrees are still of value, of course, but what stands above all else is the assurance that through our faithfulness we will receive in return the highest reward in the celestial kingdom.

Chapter 7

LESSONS FROM a
SECOND-GRADE CLASSROOM

C ome with me back to a second-grade classroom, where Miss Nelson was doing her student teaching in preparation for her graduation. I was her supervisor. Miss Nelson, looking like an experienced teacher, skillfully gained the full attention of each second grader. "Boys and girls," she began, eyes sweeping the entire group and including each child, "I'm going to tell you a story about two different neighbors, and after the story I'd like you to think about their character, or their characteristics and attributes, and be prepared to share how you feel about each one and who you would like to have as your neighbor." The children were fully engaged and listening carefully.

"There was a Mr. Brown," she began, "the friendliest man in town." She told in great detail how he knew everyone's name, including the children's, and how he would take the time to fix a broken wheel or a worn-out wagon or tricycle and make whistles from the small branches from his tree.

With a full description of Mr. Brown well implanted in the hearts and minds of the children, the teacher paused a moment, then introduced poor old Mr. Jones. Dropping her voice, and frowning slightly, she explained that everyone knew him, especially the children. Then the details of the story brought Mr. Jones to life in their minds. As children would walk past his house, they could see him through the broken picket fence sitting alone in an old chair on his porch. The only time they saw him move was when one of the older kids would dare someone to shout at him, open his gate, or throw a rock on his lawn. Then he had a very loud voice and would stand up and shake his fist.

Closing the book, Miss Nelson smiled at the children, then invited their responses regarding Mr. Brown. Much discussion followed. The enthusiastic comments from the students gave evidence of their appreciation for Mr. Brown. With the discussion nearing completion, almost as an afterthought, Miss Nelson posed the question, "Who would like to be a neighbor to Mr. Jones?"

It seemed like a strange question with no indication of a response until one second-grade boy on the back row near where I was sitting raised his hand hesitantly. Miss Nelson was obviously unprepared for anyone to express interest in being a friend to Mr. Jones. There was childish snickering throughout the classroom, but the boy with the raised hand looked straight ahead, his arm held high and his eyes on his teacher.

Something in that moment changed the mood. The snickering stopped, and the teacher simply said, "Jeff?" He lowered his hand and nervously, with all eyes on him, said hesitantly, "I wish Mr. Jones was my neighbor." Something about the way he said the words left everyone wanting to know and understand more. He went on, "I wish Mr. Jones was my neighbor because if he was my neighbor, my mom would bake a pie for me to take to him, and then he wouldn't be that way anymore."

A hush fell over the room. I watched Miss Nelson. She quickly stepped toward Jeff, gently rested her hand on his shoulder, and said almost reverently, "Thank you, Jeff, for that beautiful lesson."

I sensed the challenge of twenty-two second graders trying to give meaning to what they had experienced. I saw a young teacher lay aside her carefully prepared lesson plan to make room for a better lesson. I saw a child who was true to his conviction stand alone among his friends and make a profound statement. And then, almost as a benediction, the silence was broken by one child who spoke in a whisper just barely loud enough for all to hear, "I wish I'd said that."

The lessons I learned from a second grader have played over and over in my mind. Jeff was the teacher that day. Not the student teacher, not the regular teacher, and not the supervisor. The teacher was a second-grade boy, way ahead of many of the others. I learned several important truths from him as well.

First, remember that the obvious answer may not always be the right answer. Learn to look at things in a new way. Maybe Mr. Jones would be the best neighbor after all.

Second, dare to stand alone when you know in your heart you are right. Logic and reason may not always be reliable, but a spirit that connects to divine sources is. A child in a classroom or an adult on the witness stand can know what is right.

Third, believe in people and believe they can change. It may take a piece of pie or some other intervention, but it is possible.

Fourth, you cannot change the whole world, but your influence can change the world in which you live if you are willing to leave your comfort zone. An atmosphere of ridicule and doubt can be changed to an atmosphere of reverence by the voice of one.

Fifth, go forward with confidence that others seeking

truth will follow. When you speak truth, the Spirit will testify, and those in tune with the Spirit will respond. Some will even whisper, if not out loud, then within their hearts, "I wish I'd said that," and they will go a better way.

Elder John A. Widtsoe declared, "We need, in this Church and Kingdom, for our own and the world's welfare a group of men and women in their individual lives who shall be as a light to the nations, and . . . standards for the world to follow. Such a people must be different from the world as it now is . . . unless the world has the same aim that we have. We are here to build Zion to Almighty God, for the blessing of all the world. In that aim we are unique and different from all other peoples. We must respect that obligation, and not be afraid of it. We cannot walk as other men, or talk as other men, or do as other men, for we have a different destiny, obligation, and responsibility placed upon us, and we must fit ourselves for that great destiny and obligation" (in Conference Report, April 1940, 36).

It takes courage to stand all alone, especially in a second-grade classroom, but Jeff had been taught by his mother the power of expressing love with a home-baked pie that can change a person's feelings. "And he won't be that way anymore."

you know enough:
ponder, ask, act

Ponder

Consider all the lessons you have learned while walking
in your shoes.

Recall the lessons you have learned from others, remembering
that we are all different, but not dumb.

Remember the times you have felt inspiration.

Ask

If the glory of God is intelligence, am I meeting my potential?

Do I pray to gain insights that increase my understanding?

Do I listen with my heart and mind to the whisperings of the
Spirit?

Do I have courage to share what I know?

Do I ask for help?

Act

Make your actions consistent with your knowledge of right
and wrong.

Go forward with confidence, knowing others who seek truth
will follow.

"Seek learning even by study and also by faith" (Doctrine and
Covenants 109:7).

Seek opportunities to share with conviction what you know.

KEEPING IN
TOUCH

Chapter 8

LOVE DISCOVERED

A divorced sister with a handicapped child had moved out of the ward, I was told, because unkind things continued to be circulated about her among a few of the sisters. I asked, "How could this possibly be in a good, strong LDS ward where the sisters all seem friendly, sociable, caring, and filled with concern for one another? How could this happen?" But it had.

Destructive conversation, like a virus attacking the heart, can be life-threatening to any sister. "Did you know . . . ?" "Have you heard . . . ?" "Can you believe . . . ?" and on and on. Elder Bruce Hafen writes of this concern, "If LDS women criticize each other rather than connect with and support each other, the adversary wins the day by driving wedges into natural, womanly relationships of strength.

Because women can give so much never-failing charity to each other in relationships, one curse of the modern world has been to isolate and alienate women—including LDS women—from one another by making them more competitive" ("Women and the Moral Center of Gravity," 300).

What do the scriptures say on this matter? We read one admonition contained in the writings of Paul to Timothy: "Be thou an example of the believers in word, in conversation, in charity, in spirit, in faith, in purity" (1 Timothy 4:12). In the introduction to James 3, we are told, "By governing the tongue, we gain perfection." In James 3:10, we are counseled, "Out of the same mouth proceedeth blessing and cursing. My brethren, these things ought not so to be." This thought gives reason to ponder. Is the mouth I have used all day appropriate for my evening prayer?

In my childhood, my father took occasion to instill in my mind a lesson I shall never forget. In my heart even today I still have a recollection of the hurt when I think back on that penetrating experience.

After supper one evening during the latter part of the summer, just before harvest time, I stood with a friend on top of the big dirt mound that covered our root cellar located just next to the clothesline. Together we taunted several other girls as we pushed them down the side of the root cellar.

Kobie, my neighbor, and her cousins attempted to climb up one side as we shouted: "We're the boss of Bunker's Hill. We can fight and we can kill!" This challenging declaration, repeated in mocking tones, became a source of irritation to those below, and with increased determination they tried to get to the top and push us off. When our position looked threatened, I immediately announced that it was our root cellar anyway, and they couldn't play on it anymore! This only intensified the struggle.

The friendly chants of our other childhood activities were not part of this experience. Words were called that gave expression to troubled and mounting feelings. Kobie and her friends said we were cheating, and she called us names. I immediately reminded her that her mother was from Holland and talked funny. Someone picked up a rotten potato from the pile that had been cleared out of the root cellar and threw it, and then another potato was thrown, and another, and another, until potatoes were flying in both directions.

By now the destructive chants were being repeated first by one side and then the other, such as "Sticks and stones can break my bones, but names can never hurt me." By this time my friend and I were emerging as the winners, and Kobie and her friends were shouting through their tears. As we all left the root cellar and went our separate ways, it was an awful feeling even to be a winner.

The next day, when I had to explain to Dad why the potatoes were scattered all over the ground, he seemed to understand much more than I reported to him. He asked a lot of questions that were hard to answer. In my mind it was all Kobie's fault. Now I was in trouble, and I was determined to get even with her. My friends and I had decided we didn't need Kobie and her friends, and that was that. And so we began looking for things to justify our decision. She dressed differently. And besides, her mom talked funny. Her dad was a shoemaker who tanned smelly leather hides, while my dad was a farmer who raised turkeys.

The following evening Dad took me by the hand and we headed toward the turkey pens. I had gone with him many times before, but his silence on this occasion caused me to feel uneasy as I tried to anticipate the unknown.

We stood in silence as I watched what I had seen a few times before. One turkey was pecking on the back of the head of another one. After repeated peckings, blood came to the surface on the afflicted bird. This drew the attention of the other turkeys, who now joined in until all were pecking on the same turkey on the same wounded spot. I stared at the turkeys in silence until I felt quite uncomfortable. Then Dad broke the silence.

"Do you know why those turkeys are all pecking on that one poor turkey?" he asked. And without waiting for an answer, he continued: "It usually means they are in need of something. There may be something lacking in their diet. When that's the case, the first step is to try to give them what they need so they'll stop this terrible thing. I also have to put a tarlike salve on the wound of the injured turkey so the wound can be protected until it heals."

Dad went on, "If the other turkeys continue to peck on this bird or other birds, there is something else we can do." I listened, curious. "We can take the wounded bird out and move it away from the others so it will have a chance to heal. But the real concern is for the birds that are doing the pecking, because if they're not stopped they could destroy a whole flock of valuable turkeys. If they can't be trained, they have to be controlled." He paused. "There is a last resort."

All of a sudden, I remembered the last resort. I knew what had to happen to those birds. I had seen it done often but hadn't understood why. Months before, I had watched Dad take something that looked like electric clippers from a shelf in the turkey coop. My brother would catch one of the turkeys that had been pecking on the others. He would hold it securely under his arm while Dad seared off the sharp tip of its beak. Then my brother would release it back into the flock, now harmless because it could not peck anymore. I remembered the awful smell; I had always wondered why those dumb birds would do such a stupid thing. They deserved to have their beak tips burned off, I thought.

Dad shifted his position. He was no longer looking at the turkeys; he was looking straight at me. "Sometimes people, and not just children," he explained, "will begin to say unkind things about someone. They begin to peck on them, and then others join in the pecking. Before long a sore can develop—not one that you can see on the outside, but one that causes a lot of hurting inside. Not only does it hurt the person who is suffering such unkindness, but, even more, it can destroy the person who allows those kinds of thoughts and words to get in his head. Do you know what I mean?" he asked.

Immediately I remembered the awful feeling I had felt inside when I threw the potatoes and told Kobie and her friends to get off our root cellar and go home. Although Dad had not mentioned Kobie and the incident of that dreadful day, there was no doubt in my mind that, had it not happened, all this concern for the turkeys would never have come up.

It wasn't long after this incident that we heard that Kobie and her family were going to move to another town. A few days later I stood by the white picket fence that separated our yards and watched her dad and brothers load the truck that would carry all their belongings away. Kobie would go too, I thought, and her mom and dad. It was okay, now, that her mom spoke differently, and I remembered that she did have a beautiful singing voice, and I loved the way her dad could put soles on old shoes that would make them look new. I didn't want Kobie to go.

I wondered deep inside if I were responsible for this move, thinking of the turkeys that had to be moved to another location so their wounds could heal. And I also thought of what happened to the turkeys that didn't stop pecking the other birds.

I wanted to cry, and I wanted Kobie to stay. I wanted her to climb on our root cellar again. I wanted her to slide down our cellar door. I wanted to turn the rope for her while she jumped. But that evening Kobie and her family left their home. They left our neighborhood and our town. A lot of people gathered around to say good-bye. I just watched and watched. And when Kobie looked my way, I raised my hand just a little and waved. Kobie waved back, and somehow I hoped she knew I was sorry—very, very sorry.

I met my friend Kobie years later, after we had both gown up. We embraced and remembered and shared our love for each other as sisters in the gospel.

Whenever I hear of a relationship wounded or scarred, I remember my friend Kobie and how I felt when she moved away. I trust that as sisters in the gospel we remember our covenants to help bear one another's burdens (not add to them), to comfort those in need of comfort, and to stand as witnesses of God at all times and in all things (see Mosiah 18:8–9). May words of comfort and encouragement flow freely as we cheer for each other along our journey "home."

Chapter 9

a new FRIenD

One day, on my way home from somewhere, I made a quick stop at Costco. I needed to replenish my large candy basket for the children who regularly drop by for a little treat and a story and to sign my guest book each time they come. Heber waited in the car for me, and I took his credit card to make the purchase. I stood in line with two or three people ahead of me and several behind me. When it came my turn, the cashier explained that she could not accept my husband's credit card, which had his photo on the back. I inquired if it might be all right just this time for such a small purchase. She motioned for her supervisor, and it was agreed that I could not use that card. Fortunately I was not in a rush and didn't feel any concern except to acknowledge the wisdom in complying with the store policy.

I thanked the two who were trying to help me and left to return to the car.

A few days following this incident, a sister rang my doorbell. I didn't remember ever having seen her before. She was carrying a small white paper sack and had a warm, friendly smile. I invited her in. She began telling me the story about the day I was at Costco shopping. She told me she had been in line right behind me and had heard the conversation regarding the credit card they were not able to accept. She said after I left the candy on the counter and disappeared, the thought came to her, "I know her. Why didn't I offer to pay for the candy? It wasn't that much." But I had already gone.

This sister, whom I didn't know, handed me the small white sack. Inside were two huge, chocolate-covered strawberries. She said, "I felt sorry that I didn't think about helping you until you were out of sight. I just wanted to make it right." I immediately embraced my new friend with the deepest feelings of sincere gratitude—not so much for the delicious strawberries, which could be eaten and forgotten, but rather for the inspiring example of true sisterhood: a heart and mind that is attentive to another's circumstance. I had a delightful little visit with this very caring and thoughtful sister.

I met another sister in the temple recently who shared

with me her "therapy treatment" when she has reason for feeling "a bit restless or stressed." She told me she buys special cards when they are on sale at a nearby shop and keeps a supply on hand. "On those days when I need a lift, I go through a list of names and feel some prompting in knowing who might benefit from a thoughtful personal message from me." With a big smile, she said, "I write the cards, mail them, and feel great. I've learned that those who receive the cards say it was just what they needed that very day."

I shared with her the wise counsel I had received from Elder Marvin J. Ashton some years ago about the powerful influence for good in answering every letter and randomly sending letters, notes, or cards to those you might feel impressed to contact. He called it "a ministry by mail."

Calling upon the power within each of us to reach out and be an influence for good is an essential part of our earthly ministry. In so doing, strangers become friends, and we see the good in others. As the hymn "As Sisters in Zion" (*Hymns,* no. 309) reminds us:

> *The errand of angels is given to women;*
> *And this is a gift that, as sisters, we claim:*
> *To do whatsoever is gentle and human,*
> *To cheer and to bless in humanity's name.*

How vast is our purpose, how broad is our
   mission,
If we but fulfill it in spirit and deed.
Oh, naught but the Spirit's divinest tuition
Can give us the wisdom to truly succeed.

As sisters, daughters of God, we have power to bless the lives of others in our daily walk. Our good deeds and expressions of love, which flow when we listen to the whispering of the Spirit, can make all the difference to someone.

Chapter 10

WeBS OF FRIEnDSHIP

One of my favorite books to share with children is *Charlotte's Web,* by E. B. White. Although it is a book for children, it holds great insight into the source of joy for all of us, at every age and stage. If you have read that book, you will remember that Charlotte is the spider and Wilbur the pig. Poor Wilbur: we read that on a "dreary rainy day" he felt so "friendless, dejected, and hungry [that] he threw himself down in the manure and sobbed" (30). He felt left out, ignored, not appreciated. Have you ever had a Wilbur day? A day when you felt that alone and discouraged?

Let me remind you of how Wilbur was rescued from his plight in a way that turned sadness into joy. He was visited by Charlotte the spider, whom he hadn't liked at all when he first met her. But over the years he discovered a true friend in Charlotte, one who was willing to save his life by tirelessly spinning a beautiful web with a message that would let people know he was no ordinary pig and should not be slaughtered. Even Wilbur began to believe he was something special because his friend told him he was. "'Oh Charlotte,' he said, 'to think that when I first met you I thought you were cruel and bloodthirsty!' When he recovered from his emotion, he spoke again. 'Why did you do all this for me?' he asked. 'I don't deserve it. I've never done anything for you.'

"'You have been my friend,' replied Charlotte. 'That in itself is a tremendous thing. I wove my webs for you because I liked you. . . . By helping you, perhaps I was trying to lift up my life a trifle. Heaven knows anyone's life can stand a little of that.'" (White, *Charlotte's Web,* 164).

Maybe I relate to this story because I was raised on a farm with pigs and, yes, lots of spiders and spiderwebs in the barn. But it makes a great point: Anyone you encounter may be having a Wilbur day. What might happen if you took just a minute to spin, not a spiderweb, but a web of friendship by saying a warm "hi" to someone, maybe even a stranger?

We are all so ordinary, and yet each of us is special and unique. When we come to know that we are literally brothers and sisters in the same family, away from our heavenly home for a time, we begin to really recognize each other—not in relation to positions, possessions, prestige, or power, but rather heart to heart and soul to soul. And then, when we meet, we don't exchange just words—a wonderful exchange of the spirit takes place, spinning spiritual webs that lift us and build us and bind us to one another.

When we are engaged in spinning spiritual webs to lift each other, it is a joyful feeling. As the Lord tells us, "My spirit . . . shall enlighten your mind, which shall fill your soul with joy" (Doctrine and Covenants 11:13).

In the words of Edward Everett Hale, an American clergyman: "I am only one, but I am one. I cannot do everything, but I can do something; and what I can do, that I ought to do; and what I ought to do, by the grace of God I shall do" (as quoted in John Blaydes, comp., *The Educator's Book of Quotes,* 18).

Following a women's conference in another state where I had been asked to speak, a group of approximately five hundred sisters were gathered. It appeared that everyone was enjoying the warmth and blessing of being included, being in association with sisters older and younger, richer and poorer, some with children and some without, married and single, and all in between. It appeared to be a joyous occasion for everyone. I didn't notice anyone standing alone or appearing to be left out.

Shortly after my return home, I received a card in the

mail postmarked from that location but bearing no return address. The card had a large, colorful turtle on the front. Inside was a short message: "Thank you, Sister Kapp, for taking your precious time to look at me. So few people care nowadays." Which sister was she, I wondered, to whom such a small gesture as a kind look would make such a difference? I wanted to go back and talk with her and give her a hug and a word of encouragement. I wished I could spend a little time with just her alone, time to get to know and love her. If just to be looked at could be appreciated, I wondered if it were possible that there may have been other sisters in that large gathering who might have had a feeling of not being recognized or included or acknowledged or appreciated. Is it possible that in our daily comings and goings we might lift another with a chance word, a tap on the shoulder, or just an expression that conveys a feeling of respect and love? Maybe it is that easy to communicate a message that someone cares.

In our technology-crammed, busy world, it seems everything is on fast forward, and if we are not careful, we might miss a moment when we might be helpful. We might bypass an opportunity to be an actual instrument in the Lord's hands, even an answer to someone's prayer.

In the words of C. S. Lewis: "In Friendship . . . we think we have chosen our peers. In reality, a few years' difference in the dates of our births, a few more miles between certain houses, the choice of one university instead of another . . . the accident of a topic being raised or not raised at a first meeting—any of these chances might have kept us apart. But, for a Christian, there are, strictly speaking, no chances. A secret Master of the Ceremonies has been at work. Christ, who said to the disciples 'Ye have not chosen me, but I have chosen you,' can truly say to every group of Christian friends 'You have not chosen one another but I have chosen you for one another.' The Friendship is not a reward for our discrimination and good taste in finding one another out. It is the instrument by which God reveals to each the beauties of all the others" (*The Four Loves,* 89).

One day, following a kind act, someone may ask, "Why did you do that for me?" And you might simply answer, like Charlotte, "You have been my friend, and that in itself is a tremendous thing."

Chapter 11

A LITTLE MIRACLE

ears ago, the only telephone service that was available in my hometown—for those who could afford it—was one black telephone centrally located in the hall of a home. It was considered a luxury if you were one of the few who had a four-party line instead of a ten-party line. A private line was a thing of the future. This meant that each family on a ten-party line would be sharing the line with nine other families and would have a particular ring. Our number was three, and the ring was two longs and a short. A call could be picked up by any one of the nine other parties when they would hear our ring. The only thing that provided any privacy was the courtesy of the other members on the line to not pick up the phone unless it was their specific ring. It was apparent that curiosity generally overcame courtesy. But that was not all bad. In fact, there were some significant advantages, provided you wanted to get your message carried far and wide—or at least as far and wide as the borders of our little village.

My grandfather Leavitt arranged with the telephone company to have the central equipment located in his home. There was a switchboard in a front room of the home, with a telephone booth just inside the front entrance. Grandma Leavitt hired and trained the switchboard operators, who worked six days a week from 8:00 A.M. to 6:00 P.M. If there was ever an emergency before or after those hours, a loud ring would sound throughout the house and would be answered immediately; otherwise, the telephone office with the switchboard was closed and silent.

When Grandma, who had the instructions, was training the new operators, my cousin and I were very attentive. It was exciting to see how you could plug a cord with a metal tip into a hole on the switchboard, connecting one family, then plug in another for another family, turn a little crank that would ring in both homes, and they were connected.

Once my cousin and I used this wonderful system to solve a real crisis. Margaret and Becky, two girls we knew who really liked each other, had for some unknown reason refused to talk to each other ever again. All the kids in town were aware of the situation, and everyone had tried to persuade either one to approach the other. But each one refused to speak to the other first. This went on for days, and we all shared in the concern for this broken friendship.

One Sunday afternoon, my cousin and I took it upon ourselves to heal this friendship. We had a great idea. We crept into the telephone office in our grandma's house. We climbed up on the stool that the operator used. I plugged in one cord and rang the bell, and when Margaret, just by chance, answered the phone, I said in a very grown-up, official voice, "Just a moment, please." Then I quickly plugged in the cord connecting her friend. When Becky answered (another lucky chance), my cousin said, "Go ahead, please," in the same tone the operators used. We were each wearing a headset and sat smiling from ear to ear as we listened to the conversation.

First from Becky, "Oh, I'm so glad you called."

"I didn't call you," said Margaret, "you called me."

"No, I didn't. You called me."

"I came to the phone thinking it must be an emergency, and you were on the line."

"No, my phone rang. I picked it up, and you were on the line."

There was a long pause. "Then how *did* it happen?" they both wondered. But it didn't matter: the ice had melted, and we heard laughter. Once we knew they were really talking to each other again, we pulled both plugs and cut short their conversation.

The next day at school there was a real buzz. Margaret and Becky were telling everyone of the miracle on a Sunday when the telephone lines were closed. It was the mystery of a healed relationship. And we never told.

In the spirit of caring there is a power to heal, to mend, to restore, and to repair as we mingle with our brothers and sisters along life's path. Parley P. Pratt taught, "There is in every man a portion of the spirit of truth; a germ of light: a spiritual test or touchstone, which, if strictly observed, studied, and followed by its possessor, will witness to him; and will, as it were, leap forward with a warm glow of joy and sympathy, to every truthful spirit with which it comes in contact" (*The Essential Parley P. Pratt,* 165).

In January 2005 I received a letter that began, "Dear Sister Kapp, It feels a little strange writing a letter to you about such a brief incident long ago, but I felt prompted to write." I was interested to see what such a letter would contain:

> In the mid-1980s, I was a struggling returned missionary working at a stationery shop when one day you came into the store. I was at a very real low point in my life at the time, having recently lost my mother and my best high school friend to illnesses. Even more difficult was the struggle I was experiencing in my personal and spiritual life—I certainly qualified as one of the "walking wounded." As you

came to the counter and I rang up your purchase, we struck up a conversation. There was hardly anyone in the store, so there was no rush.

That's when something happened. I don't know what you said to me, if it was unspoken, or if you asked my name, or any of the details. But I knew from your demeanor that you sensed a need in me, and that you cared about me. There was an unspoken expression of love and confidence and concern. As you left, I remember thinking, "She knew. She knew how low I am. How could she know that?" I also felt the Spirit of the Lord.

After you left I felt uplifted not just for that day alone, but that little experience along with some others gave me the courage to continue on. I have a family now and a great life in the Church. I look back on that period and there's just a handful of things that stand out now as turning points. One of them is the brief minute with a complete stranger— a little miracle.

Let us never forget that we can be on the Lord's errand in our daily lives, participate in miracles as an instrument in His hands, and not even be aware of it. This gift is not because of who we are but because of Whose we are: His sons and His daughters.

Chapter 12

HOW I FOUND MY SISTER

as it by chance that I met my new friend Sarah Southerland? On our first acquaintance, the door opened and we began sharing thoughts, feelings, and experiences. She spoke of a special relationship that had developed in a most interesting way over an extended period of time. I asked her if she would write of the details so I could share the story with you. In response to my request, she shared this delightful account in her own words:

> Several years ago, after hearing there would be major changes made to our ward and stake, I received a phone call from the stake executive secretary asking us to please meet with the stake president that night at eight P.M. My heart sank. My husband was working full time and in school

working on his doctorate degree, and I was six months pregnant with our third child. I couldn't imagine how a calling in the bishopric would fit into our lives. I felt a small amount of relief when my husband was asked to be the executive secretary in the new bishopric. Maybe that calling wouldn't be too demanding, I thought.

The following Sunday night, after a special fireside explaining all the changes, my husband and I joined the other new bishopric members, bishops, and their families in a large room in preparation for the new leaders to be set apart. I sat next to my husband, still weeping out of a mixture of relief, concern, and pregnancy hormones, when I noticed a sister, about my age, and slightly more pregnant than myself, stand as her husband was called forward and sustained bishop of one of the newly created wards. Suddenly, my concerns about my husband seemed to fade. I could see her chasing a toddler around the room as some of the other bishops were set apart. She was at least seven months pregnant, had a toddler, and now her young husband was a bishop. I watched her face, streaked with tears but still determined to support the call the Lord had given.

The following week, whenever I began to feel overwhelmed at the sudden changes in our life, I couldn't get very blue before I would start thinking of this sweet sister. I wondered how she was doing and if she had enough support to make it through each day. I wished I could tell her how much I admired her and how often I found myself praying for her. One day, I decided to do something about it; using our stake website, I found out her name and address. I sat down and wrote out everything I had been thinking and feeling about her. I told her to remember, on those really bad, crazy, hectic, lonely days, that there was a sister in her stake who was praying for her. I signed the letter, "Love, a sister in your stake."

I sent off the letter and didn't think anything else of it. A couple of days later, while browsing at one of my favorite stores, I found a little gift and thought, "Oh! I bet my 'sister' would love that!" So I bought it and mailed it to her. A few weeks later, as I thought about motherhood and remembered some things I learned in Relief Society, I thought, "I bet my 'sister' would love to hear that!" So I wrote it down in a card and sent it. After that, it became a bit of a hobby to find cute cards and fun gifts to mail to her, always signing them, "Love, a sister in your stake."

About a year later, I started wondering if it was time to break my silence. Until that time, no one knew about the service I gave my "sister"—not even my husband! Should I tell him? Should I tell her? Should I let her know who I was and give her the chance to respond back? I thought and prayed about it until finally I decided I would at least tell my husband. On our Friday night date at a busy new restaurant in town, I decided to tell him what I had been up to. Just as I opened my mouth, my "sister" and her husband walked through the front door. I stared at them for a brief moment before bursting into tears. My husband looked at me with some amount of concern. "I think," I told him, "the Lord just answered a prayer."

My "sister" and her husband were seated only a few tables away from us. Of all the places, of all the times and days, they chose to be in the same restaurant at the same time. I knew without a doubt that it was no coincidence. The Lord was ready for me to break my silence. Tearfully, I told my husband about my "sister" and how she had miraculously just walked in the door. The next day, I wrote her a long letter describing how much it had meant to me to serve her, how I looked forward to sending cute cards and fun little gifts, and how I had truly grown to love her like a sister. This time I signed my real name and included my address and phone number. It was only later, when she wrote back, that I found out she and her husband were at the restaurant using the gift card I had sent her months earlier. How amazing is that?

My "sister" and I just celebrated our third anniversary! We get together every so often to let our kids play or to exchange recipes or share stories. I still send her cards every month, but now I have a face-to-face friend, too! While I know how much cards have meant to her, I don't think she realized how much they've meant to me! On my darkest days, when I'm feeling the worst about myself, I think of the cards and feel hope returning. "I can't be all that bad," I tell myself, "because my 'sister' thinks I'm wonderful!" It truly has blessed my life with greater happiness and I feel like the lucky one! To think of someone else's needs, to realize someone else may have had a more difficult day than me, to try to lighten the load of a fellow sister are all ways I've learned to help my day go better, my life feel more blessed, and my self-confidence blossom. I will forever be grateful for my "sister."

Thank you, Sarah Southerland, for your inspiring example of reaching beyond the boundaries of your own concerns and helping to lift the burden of another.

"As ye are desirous to come into the fold of God and to be called his people, [be] willing to bear one another's burdens, that they may be light" (Mosiah 18:8).

KEEPING IN TOUCH: PONDER, ASK, ACT

Ponder

Think about when you have felt love.
How was that love expressed?
Remember the feeling you had.

Ask

How do I express my love?
Do I understand the power of love?
What should I start doing to increase evidence of my love?
Could I weave a web of friendship that might save someone's
    life?

Act

Accept responsibility for any offenses.
Get rid of negative thoughts about anyone.
Don't throw a rotten potato.
Don't be like the turkey.
Discover ways to resolve a broken friendship.

PRINCIPLES AND PROMISES

Chapter 13

INFINITE HOPE

ope is as essential to our happiness and well-being as the air we breathe. We must keep hoping and we must keep breathing if we are to stay alive. A classic example of hope comes from the story of Molly Brown. The *New York Times* called her the "Unsinkable Molly Brown" after her dramatic experience on the ill-fated *Titanic,* which sank to the bottom of the ocean. She got in a lifeboat and began rowing. Her unwavering hope inspired others with hope.

Hope is reflected in our attitude about life, our vision of possibilities. Hope is future-oriented. It allows us to live in anticipation, to get up in the morning expecting a good day, and, if it isn't, to realize there is a tomorrow. We must not lose hope.

A most dramatic, soul-wrenching example of the need

for sustained hope in what might have appeared to be a truly hopeless situation was an account that captured the attention of nations worldwide. Every radio and TV station and all means of communication were riveted on thirty-three Chilean miners who were trapped in a deep, dark hole two thousand feet underground. For two weeks no one knew if they were dead or alive. After it was determined that they were still living, rescue efforts took another agonizingly long time, stretching their confinement to more than two months. But they never lost their hope. One nineteen-year-old miner, Jimmy Sanchez, made a correction in the report: Instead of thirty-three, there were thirty-four, because God was with them.

Hope is a gift from God that comes to us by and through the Spirit. Paul, speaking to the Romans, tells us, "We are saved by hope: but hope that is seen is not hope: for what a man seeth, why doth he yet hope for?" (Romans 8:24).

In a world filled with conflict, despair, discouragement, financial stress, political unrest, sin, suffering, and on and on, is it foolish to live with hope? Of course not. We know the reason for hope. We read in 2 Nephi 31:20, "Wherefore, ye must press forward with a steadfastness in Christ, having a perfect brightness of hope, and a love of God and of all men. Wherefore, if ye shall press forward, feasting upon the word of Christ, and endure to the end, behold, thus saith the Father: Ye shall have eternal life."

All of us live with various kinds of hope. Some hope the doctor will say, "Not malignant." Some hope the employer will say, "You're hired." Some hope the Lord will say, "You're forgiven." Hope drives us around the next corner, over the next hill, through the hot sun, and past the wintry times in our lives.

As a young child growing up on a small farm in Alberta, Canada, during the Depression years, I learned my first lesson about hope. I remember the day Dad tied a big pig in the bed of our wagon to take to the train station where it could be shipped and sold for much-needed income. I had no sense of the urgency he felt. I rode in the wagon with my mom and dad, our feet resting on the pig. When we arrived at the railroad yard to drop off the pig, much to my mom and dad's deep concern, the pig was dead. I don't remember any of the details except that my mom began crying. I remember being surprised that my mom would cry so over a dead pig, as Dad tried to comfort her. It was a mystery to me.

During the next few days, as time permitted, my mom, who had a beautiful, deep alto voice and a gift for playing the old upright piano by ear, sat at the piano singing. The music still rings in my mind today as I remember her singing, with deep feeling:

Soft as the voice of an angel,
Breathing a lesson unheard,
Hope with a gentle persuasion
Whispers her comforting word:
"Wait till the darkness is over,
Wait till the tempest is done.
Hope for the sunshine tomorrow,
After the shower is gone."
Whispering hope, oh how welcome thy voice,
Making my heart in its sorrow rejoice.

("Whispering Hope," words and music by Septimus
Winner, 1868)

My mom was filled with optimism. During those challenging times, in many situations I watched her open doors that would seem impossible.

Now, I don't suppose that any of us will ever have occasion to cry over a dead pig or be encased in a deep, dark hole for a couple of months. But we will have seasons and reasons for tears—and a reason for hope.

Hope is much more than wishful thinking. The principle or doctrine of hope draws us forward with a sense of optimism and anticipation, giving us an eternal perspective to envision the light at the end of the tunnel. The promise is realized when we choose to follow the path, however steep, leading to our ultimate destination, our eternal home.

Because we are mortal and the plan provides for agency, sometimes we make some unwise or wrong choices. We may feel guilty or unworthy of the things we hope for. Reviewing our list of shortcomings, we may begin to lose hope. That would be the desire of Satan. And he is always there if there is a chance we would be tempted to lose hope, to give in, give up, or give out.

It is not God's plan that we should be perfect before we can experience this priceless gift of hope. It is in our imperfections and our dependence upon God and His mercy that we find our reason for hope.

The trials and tests in our lives are not to discourage us but to refine us, teaching us that we must call upon the Lord. They are not to weaken us but to strengthen us. They are not to destroy us but to sanctify us, to help us become more Christlike, more loving, more forgiving, and more optimistic.

If the morning newscast, the daily newspaper, or the challenges of our day cause us to lose hope, we must repent. We must change our mind. Hope is a catalyst for repentance and change. We can choose faith in place of fear, hope in place of doubt, and charity in place of contention.

In Ether 12:4 we read this touching, comforting message: "Wherefore, whoso believeth in God might with surety hope for a better world, yea, even a place at the right hand of

God, which hope cometh of faith, maketh an anchor to the souls of men."

I testify of that promise. There was a time in my life when my hope was severely tested, almost to the point of giving up. I think it is safe to say that most of us, maybe all of us, can relate to that feeling. I'm sure there are those among us who are experiencing a severe test at this time, trying to hang on when it seems that no one understands, not even our Father in Heaven.

But there is someone who not only understands but knows us and knows how we feel. Speaking of the Son of God, Alma testified: "And he shall go forth, suffering pains and afflictions and temptations of every kind . . . that he may know according to the flesh how to succor his people according to their infirmities" (Alma 7:11–12).

For many years after our marriage in the temple, every month my husband and I lived with great hope and anticipation. And every month we had a great letdown. Those highs and lows became even worse as my younger sister called eleven times over the years to tell me she was expecting one more baby.

For years, as well-meaning people would ask me the familiar question, "How many children do you have?" I would try to respond in a tone of hope, "Not any yet." Sometimes even now I give the same answer, "Not any yet," and I get a smile in return, suggesting that I might think I could be blessed like Elizabeth in the Bible in her old age.

When I have times of discouragement, when answers to earnest prayers seem not heard or delayed for one reason or another and I don't understand, I try to see myself in the center of a triangle. The base of the triangle is the rock-solid foundation representing the infinite and intimate Atonement of Jesus Christ. He gave His life for you and for me individually. It is difficult to try to comprehend the profound blessing of the Atonement, but we know that the Atonement is at the very heart of our salvation and exaltation, our infinite and ultimate hope. That foundation is there for you and for me. It is this foundation that Helaman was speaking about to his sons: "And now, my sons, remember, remember that it is upon the rock of our Redeemer, who is Christ, the Son of God, that ye must build your foundation; that when the devil shall send forth his mighty winds, yea, his shafts in the whirlwind, yea, when all his hail and his mighty storm shall beat upon you, it shall have no power over you to drag you down to the gulf of misery and endless wo, because of the rock upon which ye are built, which is a sure foundation, a foundation whereon if men build they cannot fall" (Helaman 5:12).

One side of the triangle is faith in the Lord Jesus Christ. The other side is charity, the pure love of Christ. And looking heavenward, at the peak of the triangle is hope. Infinite hope.

Hope is a link to both faith and charity. With faith, we overcome fear. When our faith may waver for whatever reason, hope is like the mortar between the bricks that holds them together. The more hope we feel, the greater our faith. The stronger our hope, the greater our charity. The triangle of hope is like impenetrable armor protecting us. And there will be times when we need that protection.

My father and I were very close all my life. During the last stages of his stomach cancer, when his spirit had literally outgrown his body, and his graduation, as he called it, was very near, I learned more about hope. We talked about how much we were going to miss each other when the call came to return home. He said to me with deep conviction, "You know, Ardie, it gets really exciting when you get near the infield." He had no fears, just anticipation. He had kept the commandments, followed the promptings of the Spirit, and received the promise of the blessings of the temple ordinances and covenants, and he was ready to return home. He was full of anticipation. He radiated a spirit of hope.

Now, I don't think we need to be at death's door to feel that spirit. The spirit of hope is reflected in our countenances, in the tone of our voices, in the words we speak, in our interactions with others, and in the things we choose to discuss or not to discuss.

Let us make a list, a prioritized list, of our most earnest hopes, and then repeat often the words so familiar to Latter-day Saints everywhere:

> *When dark clouds of trouble hang o'er us*
> *And threaten our peace to destroy,*
> *There is hope smiling brightly before us,*
> *And we know that deliv'rance is nigh.*
>
> ("We Thank Thee, O God, for a Prophet,"
> *Hymns,* no. 19)

Our prophets and Church leaders are indeed great examples of hope. Knowing a bit about President Dieter F. Uchtdorf's childhood and the extreme conditions in Germany following World War II, one might wonder how, under such severe tests and trials, he developed his optimism and hope. He tells us of his understanding of this great gift.

"Hope is a gift of the Spirit. It is a hope that through the Atonement of Jesus Christ and the power of His Resurrection, we shall be raised unto life eternal and this because of our faith in the Savior. This kind of hope is both a principle of promise as well as a commandment, and, as with all commandments, we have the responsibility to make it an active part of our lives and overcome the temptation to lose hope. Hope in our Heavenly Father's merciful plan of happiness leads to peace, mercy, rejoicing, and gladness. The hope of salvation is like a protective helmet; it is the foundation of our faith and an anchor to our souls" ("The Infinite Power of Hope," 21–22).

Through our covenants with our Father in Heaven and His Son, Jesus Christ, and with the gift of the Holy Ghost, we have reason for infinite hope today and to the very end of our lives. As we renew our covenants each Sabbath day and covenant to take upon us His name and keep His commandments, we can have His Spirit to be with us (see Doctrine and Covenants 20:77, 79).

Infinite hope is a gift of the Spirit. May we all seek earnestly for this precious gift.

Chapter 14

WITHIN THESE VERY WALLS

As with most classic childhood stories, there is a moral woven within the fabric of the story of the three little pigs that remains long after childhood has passed. As the story goes, one of the little pigs had built his house of straw, thinking that would be quick and easy. The second little pig took more time to build his house of sticks—much safer than straw, he must have thought. The third little pig had another plan. He built his house of brick on a sure foundation.

The big bad wolf had a plan of his own. He did not hide it; the intent of his message was clear: "I'll huff and I'll puff and I'll blow your house down!" His huff and his puff included his total commitment to his destructive plan.

The house made of straw was quickly destroyed. The house made of sticks may have been stronger than the one made of straw, but it also fell under the destructive force of the enemy. The little pigs had to run for their lives.

The big bad wolf never gave up. He was prepared to go after the beautiful brick home and the residents within its walls. Fortunately, the foundation, the construction, the architectural design, and all the plans had been carefully prepared to allow the brick house to endure and survive any opposition that might come from the dangerous huff and puff of the big bad wolf. And, as the story goes, the huff and the puff of the big bad wolf could not penetrate the walls made of brick. The house stood safe against the invading danger and was, in fact, the setting where the wolf lost his life and the three little pigs were safe and probably lived happily ever after.

But, make no mistake, the huffing and the puffing of the big bad wolf in an effort to destroy our homes and families is ever present. The crucial question for each of us is this: Will our houses stand and be a refuge, a safe place, a protection against the powers of the evil one? Today we are faced with the terrible, destructive, constant forces of the adversary. Our homes are under attack. With concern for the safety and protection of our families, we may put smoke detectors in our ceilings, double-paned glass in our windows, and security locks on our doors, along with alarm mechanisms that could alert the police in case of an attempted break-in.

But, in the words of Elder L. Tom Perry: "We need to make our homes a place of refuge from the storm, which is increasing in intensity all about us. Even if the smallest openings are left unattended, negative influences can penetrate the very walls of our homes" ("The Importance of the Family," 40).

How strong are the spiritual foundations of our homes? Are those homes built of straw or wood that could not stand the opposition of our day? What do we have on the walls of our homes today that might serve as a reminder to family members of the blessings promised to us when we work together to build a strong foundation?

On the outer wall at the entrance of the Cardston Alberta Temple is a bronze plaque with the following message written by Orson F. Whitney:

> *Hearts must be pure to come within these walls,*
> *Where spreads a feast unknown to festive halls.*
> *Freely partake, for freely God has given,*
> *And taste the holy joys that tell of heaven.*
> *Here learn of Him who triumphed o'er the grave*
> *And unto man the keys, the kingdom gave.*
> *Joined here by powers, the past and present bind*
> *The living and the dead perfection find.*

Within these sacred walls, love abounds, feelings are tender, hearts are softened, relationships are strengthened, and the desire to express tender thoughts and feelings reaches beyond the veil. A power for goodness and love is felt. The temple is truly a safe place.

Obedience to temple covenants comes with a promise of blessings in our homes and in our lives now and forever. Although we cannot still the storms that rage outside the temple or outside our homes, attending the temple can strengthen us and greatly affect what goes on inside our homes and hearts.

Home is the place where we learn the language of love, where we speak kind words, where hearts are softened, and where thoughts and words and conversation prepare us with the spiritual strength to guard against the threats and influences of the world.

Home is where family rules are established, boundaries are set, and "growing up" takes place in a safe environment. It is a place where the boundaries are sometimes tested and the rules questioned, where resistance is tempered and discipline provides for the growing-up process to develop.

A number of years ago I was directing and producing educational programs for the Utah Network for Instructional Television. It was at that time that I gained a deeper appreciation for the need to control what goes on inside the walls of our homes if growing is to take place. I had arranged to do a TV program for third-grade students that would be broadcast to classrooms throughout the state. It would help children learn about the importance of a proper environment where there are regulations and rules and standards that must be kept.

I had two third-grade students with me on location for the filming of the program. We visited a chicken hatchery. The cameraman had everything set up, and the owner of the chicken hatchery took time to explain to the children who were with me and also those who would later watch the program the process for little chickens to hatch out of eggs. He allowed the children to assist him in placing a number of ordinary-looking eggs in a large incubator, explaining that the drawer holding the eggs provided a safe place, like the walls of their homes. He explained that the hatching would take place in about twenty-one days. The children filled with anticipation for the day we were to return. We marked the calendar, and on the twenty-first day we returned to the hatchery.

The television camera was set up and the lens adjusted to allow for close observation. The children were wide-eyed and full of excitement. The drawer was carefully pulled open where the eggs had been placed. There was much commotion going on inside. A miracle had taken place. There were many little chicks in all different stages of development, some ahead of the others. Some were free from their shells, and their downy feathers were dry and fluffy. Others just out of the shell were still wet, with the down sticking to their delicate little bodies. Curiously, I picked up one of the eggs that showed no sign of change. The shell that held that little chicken captive would have had to be very strong to withstand the energy and activity I could feel going on inside it. Why was this little chicken not out of the shell like the others? I asked the owner if I might use my fingernail to remove a bit of the shell very gently and carefully so we could observe the effort within. He hesitated a minute, then agreed, explaining, "You realize, of course, that if you break the shell and relieve the pressure, that little chicken will likely die." The very thought stopped me immediately, and I carefully placed the egg back in the drawer of the incubator. "Yes," he went on, "all the effort, the struggle, the activity that you feel going on inside the shell is essential for the little chicken's development and survival. It is through this struggle to break out of the shell that the chicken develops the strength to survive." I realized then the help I wanted to give the chicken to make its way easier could actually cause its death. But the incubator, the safe environment, the safe place, was managed by the owner.

And so it is within the very walls of our homes where growing up must take place. The environment is managed by dedicated parents. The lessons learned, sometimes under great difficulty and resistance, will require patience and much love before the hatching takes place. Our homes, like a protective incubator, are the safe places with controlled environments where lessons are learned, discipline provided, boundaries held firm, challenges overcome, and obedience practiced.

President George Q. Cannon wrote of the power that we can have within our homes: "By the Saints refusing to be led by the influences of Satan and not yielding to his seductive temptations, he is virtually bound so far as they are concerned; and, when the head of the family can attain unto this power and persuade his wife and family to do likewise, the power of Satan will be bound in that habitation, and the Millennium will have commenced in that household; and, if all should take this course, man and the earth would soon be prepared for the coming of Jesus and the ushering in of the full millennial glory and the complete binding of Satan, all of which glory they would already have a foretaste" (*Gospel Truth,* 88).

> *Home can be a heav'n on earth*
> *When we are filled with love,*
> *Bringing happiness and joy,*
> *Rich blessings from above—*
> *Warmth and kindness, charity,*
> *Safety and security—*
> *Making home a part of heaven,*
> *Where we want to be.*

Praying daily in our home,
We'll feel His love divine;
Searching scriptures faithfully,
We'll nourish heart and mind.
Singing hymns of thanks, we'll say,
"Father, help us find the way
Leading to our home in heaven,
Where we long to stay."

("Home Can Be a Heaven on Earth,"
Hymns, no. 298)

Good homes, like spiritual incubators, provide a safe place to return to again and again, where the power of love is ever present.

Chapter 15

HE KNOWS US PERSONALLY

One of the most important principles and promises of our Father's plan is that of personal revelation. Our mission in life, for each one of us, is personal. I pray for the assistance of the Holy Ghost for me—and for you—to help us increase our understanding and enlarge our capacity to benefit from this remarkable gift.

Personal revelation requires that our Father in Heaven know us personally. He knows our names and our personal challenges. He knows what we have the power to become. He knows the influence we can be in making not just a difference but a profound difference—not in the entire world, perhaps, but within our circle of influence.

We know that our birth at this particular time was foreordained in the eternities. We have a foreordained mission.

It is according to the grand eternal plan that we are walking the path of mortality at this time and in this place. The Lord is counting on each one of us.

With that realization, you might go out some starry night, look up into the grandeur of the sky, and ponder, "Why me? Why now? Why here? Am I doing what I came to do? Am I on course, or do I need a little course correction?" Yes, of course we need course corrections! But that is no reason to become discouraged. We are bound to make mistakes, to have disappointments and feelings of failure. That is part of mortality, and no one can escape it. But, thankfully, there are ways provided for us to make course corrections, to change who we are to who we may become—living with joy and anticipation, with an eternal perspective and sweet assurance.

Consider these powerful words from Elder M. Russell Ballard to the women of the Church. Hear them as if he were speaking to you personally:

"More than ever before we need women of faith, virtue, vision. . . . We need women who can hear and who will respond to the voice of the Lord, women who at all costs will defend and protect the family. . . . We do need women who rejoice in their womanhood and have a spiritual confirmation of their identity, their value, and their eternal destiny. Above all, we need women who will stand up for truth and righteousness and decry evil at every turn and simply say, 'Lord, here am I, send me'" ("Women of Righteousness," 72–73).

Today, more than any other time in history, the world needs women who know the Lord and know themselves—women who will take a stand. It is no wonder Satan tries to deceive, confuse, and distract women in any way possible. Women, particularly mothers, are at the very heart of the great plan of happiness. The battle between right and wrong, between good and evil, is real and increasing. We know it will accelerate. Satan has marshaled his forces for the last great battle. And this is our time—the time for us to be prepared in every way possible to receive the whisperings of the Spirit in our minds and in our hearts. Many are counting on us.

Let us consider five principles relating to personal revelation—this glorious gift that allows you and me to be in communication with our Father in Heaven when we choose to follow the path.

1. God is our Father and we are all His children.
2. The Holy Ghost communicates in many ways.
3. Communication involves talking, listening, and remembering.
4. Learning to listen and to trust is essential.
5. You can receive personal revelation.

God Is Our Father and We Are His Children

Think of that! When we sense this true relationship, it helps us realize who we really are: daughters of our Heavenly Father who loves us. He wants us to understand that He is our beloved Father and that we are His daughters. President Boyd K. Packer is speaking to each of us when he tells us, "It is critically important that you understand . . . that you're innately, inherently, and intuitively good. When you say, 'I can't! I can't solve my problems!' I want to thunder out, 'Don't you realize who you are? Haven't you learned yet that you are a son or a daughter of Almighty God? Do you not know that there are powerful resources inherited from Him that you can call upon to give you steadiness and courage and great power?'" ("Self-Reliance," 88).

Every child of God upon the earth is given the light of Christ and can receive promptings, impressions, and guidance. But for members of The Church of Jesus Christ of Latter-day Saints, there is more. By the authority and power of the holy priesthood, after the baptism of water, we receive the gift of the Holy Ghost. This is the key to personal revelation. Revelation is communication from the Father and the Son through the third member of the Godhead, the Holy Ghost. He is the messenger. Just think, we can have the companionship of a member of the Godhead with us in our daily lives. Can we ever conceive of a greater blessing?

When Joseph Smith was asked how the Church was different from other contemporary religions, he responded that the distinction lay in the Church's method of baptism and in the gift of the Holy Ghost, and "that all other considerations were contained in [that gift]" (*Teachings: Joseph Smith,* 97).

So how do we receive this message in today's busy, noisy, high-tech world? Is it by text messaging, or some satellite connection?

The Holy Ghost Communicates with Us in Many Ways

In the Doctrine and Covenants we read these words that give clarity to this divine line of communication with our Heavenly Father. He tells us: "Yea, behold, I will tell you in your mind and in your heart, by the Holy Ghost, which shall come upon you and which shall dwell in your heart" (Doctrine and Covenants 8:2).

I think the mind has to do with our thoughts, and the heart encompasses our feelings. I have learned that if we will remember our Lord and Savior Jesus Christ, keep His commandments, and take upon us His name, His promise to us is that we can always have His Spirit to be with us. What more could we ever want? As we learn to listen, the message may come to us from what we see, what we hear, or what we feel. And if we are not attuned to the Spirit, we may not feel or recognize its promptings.

What course correction or change are we willing to make? What things might we be willing to give up or change so we can have that companionship always?

Communication Involves Talking, Listening, and Remembering

We are anxious to know the answers to our questions and receive guidance, but sometimes we fail to take our specific questions to our Father in Heaven in prayer. Over and over in the scriptures we are encouraged to ask. "Ask, and ye shall receive; knock, and it shall be opened unto you" (Doctrine and Covenants 88:63). President Packer tells us, "No message appears in scripture . . . more ways than, 'Ask, and ye shall receive'" ("Reverence Invites Revelation," 21). What might be different if, in our daily prayers, we were to ask for help in receiving the promptings that would guide us throughout the day, every day?

The Bible Dictionary states that there are "blessings that God is already willing to grant, but that are made conditional on our asking for them" (Bible Dictionary, s.v. "Prayer,"

753). Is it possible that some blessings are being withheld because we fail to ask or because we don't take the time to listen or to follow through on the impressions we have received?

Can you remember the number of times you have been prompted to make a call, write a note, or visit a friend? Perhaps something occurred that you may have thought was a coincidence, not realizing that you were an instrument in the Lord's hands in answer to another's prayer. Remember the times when you took a turn in the road, only to realize the decision was of significant importance, maybe changing a job, selling your home, or moving to a new location? Or perhaps the time you received a calling and felt overwhelmed and then a quiet peace filled your whole soul? Remember when you asked in earnest prayer and went forward in faith, and then, looking back in the days or years later, you could see how the Lord's hand had guided and directed your life when you may have felt you were on your own? There are times when we must walk by faith as far as the light shines and then even take one step into the dark.

Often, if we are to receive personal revelation, we have a part to play. We may need to study it out in our own mind and then take it to the Lord in prayer. Sometimes we feel that it is right, or we feel unsettled, or sometimes we may not feel anything. Maybe that choice doesn't really matter. I take comfort in the words of Elder Dallin H. Oaks: "When a choice will make a difference in our lives . . . and when we are living in tune with the Spirit and seeking divine guidance, we can be sure that we will receive the guidance we need to attain righteous goals. The Lord will not leave us unassisted when a choice is important to our eternal welfare" (*The Lord's Way,* 38).

The Lord promises, "Pray always, and I will pour out my Spirit upon you" (Doctrine and Covenants 19:38). Just after I had been called to serve as the Young Women general president, I remember vividly how I yearned for a direct line of communication immediately. I had lots of questions and felt an urgent need for immediate answers. Of course, it wasn't the first time I had prayed with real intent, but I remember on that occasion how the immediate answer came.

I was reading the Book of Mormon in Alma 37:36–37, and the words came as personal revelation to me. I marked that date in the margin of my scriptures and drew strength from those verses during those eight years of service—and still do. I heard those words in my mind and in my heart. "Cry unto God for all thy support. . . . Counsel with the Lord in all thy doings, and he will direct thee for good." I testify that there is great peace that comes from counseling with the Lord.

Learning to Listen and to Trust Is Essential

The lines of a poem that my sister Shirley wrote for her eleven children has become a motto for our family that we repeat over and over again:

Listen to your inner drummer, step to its quiet beat.
The world beats another rhythm, a rhythm of defeat.
Let us become a holy people, peculiar and divine.
Living in the world but walking out of time.

In today's world, we as women, you and I, must take a stand and march to a different drumbeat if we are to defend those values and principles that are most precious. We will be guided and directed, prompted and inspired. Our position may not always be popular. I remember on one occasion when I felt to take a stand that was not popular initially. The leader of the committee spoke to me privately following the meeting and explained, "You have courage, but you lack judgment." Of course I felt uncomfortable, until a couple of weeks later when my recommendation had proven right after all.

There may be times in our lives—for whatever reason—when we may wonder if our prayers are being heard, or if the communication line is down. Maybe we feel we are not worthy or that our Father doesn't care or has forgotten us. At such a time the adversary would relish the possibility of infecting us with doubt and fear. We must not let this happen. There is too much at stake.

I testify that the channel of communication with our Father through the Holy Ghost is never closed unless we ourselves close it.

You Can Receive Personal Revelation

"Listen to the voice of Jesus Christ, your Redeemer, the Great I Am, whose arm of mercy hath atoned for your sins; who will gather his people even as a hen gathereth her chickens under her wings, even as many as will hearken to my voice and humble themselves before me, and call upon me in mighty prayer" (Doctrine and Covenants 29:1–2).

Here we have the key to personal revelation. Hearken (listen) and pray. Yes, in the bright sunlight of the day, and even in our darkest hours, He is there for you and for me.

Chapter 16

STOP, LOOK, and LISTEN

In my hometown on the wide-open prairie in Alberta, Canada, we had a population of three hundred people. My husband teases me by saying that was only at Christmastime, when people came home for the holidays. At the far west end of town, which was only a few miles from the east end, we had a connection with the outside world by way of the Canadian Pacific Railway. The train passed through our town of Glenwood three times a week.

It became a sort of ritual to listen for the forlorn sound of the train whistle in the far distance. The sound of the train would get louder and louder until you could also hear the wheels on the tracks as it sometimes whizzed by and sometimes stopped. The road that ran straight west in front of our house made it possible to see the train as it went by at what seemed like an incredible speed. At the side of the road next to the track was a very large sign that read STOP, LOOK, AND LISTEN. We were told as children that it was to secure our safety by warning us that the train was coming. And if we did not stop, look both ways, and listen, we could get run over and lose our lives.

An old man by the name of Bert Giles who lived in our town was riding his bike one late afternoon when he was run over by the train and killed. The whole town was in shock; it was a sad day for everyone. We asked: "Did he not remember the sign?" That day Mr. Giles must not have seen the train coming, and he must not have heard the whistle.

It was that day as a child that I began to realize the importance of the sign, STOP, LOOK, AND LISTEN. And that simple, clear direction continues to grow in importance as the train of life in our high-tech world accelerates. The technology of our day is almost unbelievable. When I was a child, it was unimaginable that someday you might have a small piece of equipment you could carry in the palm of your hand with your own telephone number on a private line, not to mention being able to call to distant places throughout the world. Unthinkable! And a computer that could send an e-mail to the other side of the world in seconds was mythological, to say the least.

And now it is a fact. It is our time—and what a grand

time it is. We have reason to rejoice, but only if during our journey on this fast-moving train we discipline ourselves to STOP, LOOK, AND LISTEN.

One day we may be asked to respond to several significant questions by the One to whom we owe our very lives:

- Did you take time to stop?
- Did you take time to look?
- Did you take time to listen?
- Did you take time to remember?
- Did you take time to give thanks?
- What do you remember from your mortal journey, where you were given eyes to see and ears to hear and a heart to know and feel?

In our busy days, we carry our laptops, cell phones, game boards, and such with us and then return home to pick up our e-mails and messages on our voice mail, catch a quick bite from the microwave, and turn on the TV to catch up on the latest news in our overcrowded lives. We can record one TV program while watching another and read condensed books and add more and more appointments to our calendars and realize the summer is gone and life is passing and we're out of control.

I believe the adversary would, if possible, try to keep us busily engaged in a multitude of ever good things if we could be distracted from the few things that make all the difference. President Spencer W. Kimball said, "Since immortality and eternal life constitute the sole purpose of life, all other interests and activities are but incidental thereto" (*The Miracle of Forgiveness*, 2).

You might ask yourself, When do I take time to ponder? When do I take time not just to look but to see? When do I take time not only to listen but to hear the voice of a child, the sound of a bird, the whispering of the Spirit in my mind and heart?

We see in the words of Nephi in the Book of Mormon a great pattern that serves as a guide. He begins, "For it came to pass after I had desired to know the things that my father had seen, . . . I sat pondering in mine heart," and after some time he says, "The Spirit said unto me: Look!" Each time Nephi took time to look, he was given a vision and the angel asked again, "What desirest thou?" and again the admonition came to *look,* and he was allowed to see the things his father saw, which was his desire. He stopped. He sat pondering, he looked, and he heard the voice of the Lord (see 1 Nephi 11:1, 8, 10).

President Henry B. Eyring spoke of his commitment to write down the things he wanted to remember. He said, "I heard in my mind—not in my own voice—these words: 'I'm not giving you these experiences for yourself. Write them down.' . . . Before I would write, I would ponder this question: 'Have I seen the hand of God reaching out to touch us or our children or our family today?'" ("O Remember, Remember," 66–67).

The "journal-keeping" of Nephi, of Alma, and especially the tremendous efforts of Mormon were motivated by their wish to keep future generations always in remembrance. How often in the Book of Mormon do we read of God delivering a group of people when they were faithful, when they *remembered?* How important is it for each of us to remember those times when, without the Lord's help, we could never have accomplished the mission or the calling, the task or the challenge given to us?

When Oliver Cowdery began his labors as a scribe in the translation of the Book of Mormon, the Lord spoke to him through Joseph Smith as follows:

"Verily, verily, I say unto you, if you desire a further witness, cast your mind upon the night that you cried unto me in your heart, that you might know concerning the truth of these things.

"Did I not speak peace to your mind concerning the matter? What greater witness can you have than from God?" (Doctrine and Covenants 6:22–23).

It is as if the Lord were saying: "Remember, remember, Oliver, what I told you before. Treasure those memories.

Draw strength from them, and never, ever forget." He could say to each of us: "Remember those times when I spoke peace to your mind."

Alma tells us: "Awake and arouse your faculties" (Alma 32:27). This requires some work and attention on our part. It is not always easy. We may look but not see with an eye of faith. We may listen but not hear the whisperings of the Spirit because other noise interferes. We may touch but be "past feeling" (1 Nephi 17:45). We may live but without sensitivity—and thus our arsenal of memory is not filled with experiences that can be used to fight against doubt, fear, discouragement, despair, or even faltering faith.

When we are so busily engaged and consumed that our minds are clogged, saturated, or preoccupied, and we are distracted in our thoughts, with no time to ponder, we may see the evidence of God's hand but forget the Creator.

Is it possible to be dead spiritually while we are still alive physically? When we take control of our lives, our schedules, our plans, and our appointments, prioritizing according to our values and our goals, we will experience things we would have otherwise missed. President Dieter F. Uchtdorf gives us this inspiring counsel: "Let us simplify our lives a little. Let us make the changes necessary to re-focus our lives on the sublime beauty of the simple, humble path of Christian discipleship—the path that leads always toward a life of meaning, gladness, and peace" ("Of Things That Matter Most," 22).

Some days we are sure to feel that we are on a fast-moving train. But with the assurance that the train we are traveling on is built to stay on the straight and narrow track and we are committed to stay on board, we will be sure to reach our destination having had an eventful, challenging, and glorious ride.

PRINCIPLES AND PROMISES: PONDER, ASK, ACT

Ponder

Hope is more than wishful thinking.

Consider the battle between right and wrong that is raging,
and your own preparation to face it.

Ask

Am I prepared to face the battle?

Am I using the ammunition, the principles that secure the
promises?

How firm is my foundation? Does it need reinforcement in
some places for the benefit of me and my family?

Do I take time to ponder and listen to the Spirit?

Act

Know the correct principles and govern yourself.

Prepare to make and keep sacred covenants.

Build on a firm foundation.

Pray always.

Trust in the Lord.

GOD'S LOVE

Chapter 17

my soul delighteth in god's love

As I share some thoughts concerning God's uncondi-tional love for each one of us, my desire is that the Spirit will testify to you in your mind and in your heart that you truly are a beloved daughter of our Heavenly Father held back to come forth at this very time. He is counting on us, not only to experience His love, but to be instruments in His hands to share His love.

This assurance is critical if we are to have the strength, the confidence, and the courage to stand up against the in-creasing influences of the adversary. He would, if possible, have us question our divine nature and our individual worth.

To feel God's love is to feel valued, accepted, and ap-preciated for who we are and what we have the capability of becoming. When we choose to follow His path, no blessing will be denied.

Elder Dallin H. Oaks tells us, "The love of God does not supersede His laws and His commandments, and the effect of God's laws and commandments does not diminish the purpose and effect of His love" ("Love and Law," 26). Sometimes it is easier to focus on God's laws and commandments than on His love for us. Because we are mortal and make mistakes and feel that we never quite measure up to our goals, we may have a tendency to lose hope and confidence at difficult times. These are the very times when we must draw ourselves away from the world and the influences of the adversary. We must turn in prayer to our Father who knows our needs and our feelings and wants to communicate with us. He tells us, "Draw near unto me and I will draw near unto you; seek me diligently and ye shall find me; ask, and ye shall receive; knock, and it shall be opened unto you" (Doctrine and Covenants 88: 63).

On November 10, 2010, at a worldwide satellite broadcast, the Young Women values were introduced. The first of those values, which has been repeated over and over again, was as follows: "Faith: I am a daughter of a Heavenly Father who loves me. I will have faith in His eternal plan, which centers in Jesus Christ, my Savior." This helps clarify my true identity, who I am and Whose I am. My Father loves me and has a plan to bless me. Our Savior gave His life for me.

Coming to grasp even in part the magnitude and the significance of the Atonement and the Savior's love for every child of God gives meaning, hope, promise, and purpose to life. He went all the way through the Garden of Gethsemane to the cross and paid the price so that we might receive all the blessings of God when we use our agency and choose to follow His great plan of happiness.

President George Q. Cannon, a counselor to three prophets, helps us grasp an insight into this remarkable relationship:

"Now, this is the truth. We humble people, we who feel ourselves sometimes so worthless, so good-for-nothing, we are not so worthless as we think. There is not one of us but what God's love has been expended upon. There is not one of us that He has not cared for and caressed. There is not one of us that He has not desired to save and that He has not devised means to save. There is not one of us that He has not given His angels charge concerning. We may be insignificant and contemptible in our own eyes and in the eyes of others, but the truth remains that we are the children of God and that He has actually given His angels—invisible beings of power and might—charge concerning us, and they watch over us and have us in their keeping" (*Gospel Truth,* 3–4).

When we choose to follow the Spirit and do what is right, we have guardian angels watching over us. "For I will go before your face. I will be on your right hand and on your left, and my Spirit shall be in your hearts and mine angels round about you to bear you up" (Doctrine and Covenants 84:88).

When we come to an understanding of our true identity as daughters of God, women of the covenant, knowing what is expected of us, we join a mighty force for righteousness. We experience our Savior's love and prepare to share His love with others. We become instruments in His hands. When we learn to listen to the promptings of the Spirit, we discover a natural desire, a yearning to reach out to others.

Is the capacity to be a true disciple and show love for everyone a gift that anyone might possess, or is it reserved for just a few? Elder John H. Groberg explains: "What then is the common denominator that covers all men and all women over all time and all circumstances? The amount of love they choose to develop in their hearts! Everyone is on equal footing to achieve that, to whatever degree they desire. All they need to do is first love God with all their hearts, minds, and souls, and then move on to its earthly expression by loving their neighbor as themselves (see Matthew 22:35–40)" (*The Other Side of Heaven,* 279).

That love would put an end to judging one another,

criticizing, gossiping, ignoring, rejecting, avoiding, and many other ills. When we are prepared in our hearts to love, we will have opportunities to be answers to others' prayers. President Thomas S. Monson tells us, "The sweetest experience in mortality is to know that our Heavenly Father has worked through us" (Swinton, *To the Rescue,* front jacket flap).

When we were baptized members of The Church of Jesus Christ of Latter-day Saints, hands were placed on our heads by men having priesthood authority, and we were given the greatest gift in this mortal life: the gift of the Holy Ghost, a gift given to strengthen us, guide us, comfort us, warn us, teach us, and communicate messages from our Father in Heaven. When we are blessed to have His Spirit with us, regardless of the situation, we can feel His love. When we open our hearts and turn to Him in faith and prayer, we need never feel alone. He is always there. He tells us, "Peace I leave with you, my peace I give unto you: not as the world giveth, give I unto you. Let not your heart be troubled, neither let it be afraid" (John 14:27). There are times when the feelings of love and peace in the most difficult circumstances may not be explained but cannot be denied.

President Harold B. Lee said: "Sisters, walk by the spirit of revelation. Let the Holy Spirit's promptings guide you night and day, fill your soul with love and guard you from harm, protect you from evil and make you keenly sensitive to the impressions of the Holy Spirit. You lovely sisters, tuned as you are with the fineness of woman's intuitive nature, more finely tuned than men in most instances if you'll learn to give heed to those promptings of the Holy Spirit and then follow them, you'll find those things that are presented to your mind [will come] true very shortly thereafter. If you'll learn to follow your impressions, you'll be amazed to see how you'll walk daily by the spirit of revelation. Now, every one of you is blessed to receive that. Draw heavily upon it, keep yourselves in tune by living the gospel, keep free from criticism, from bitterness, and from frictions that otherwise would make you unfit for this service, and the Lord will bless you and you will be amply rewarded" (*The Teachings of Harold B. Lee,* 424).

We are the children of God. He is our Father. May we each carry within our hearts the feeling of God's unconditional love so we may have a desire, a yearning, to reach out to share that love with all our brothers and sisters.

Chapter 18

PRESS FORWARD WITH STEADFASTNESS IN CHRIST

As a child in Primary, I remember standing and singing with my whole heart and soul, "Jesus wants me for a sunbeam, To shine for him each day" (*Children's Songbook,* 60). I remember thinking that He really needed me. And I remember how I felt deep inside, singing, "I'll be a sunbeam for him," and then thinking, I can if I but try. He still needs us to shine for him each day, every day. We can if we but try. And we will try.

This is our time to "arise and shine forth, that [our] light may be a standard for the nations" (Doctrine and Covenants 115:5). The heavens are very much open to women today. They are not closed unless we ourselves, by our choice, close them.

In a time past when the adversary sought to destroy the

purposes of God and lead people astray, Captain Moroni raised the standard of liberty and fearlessly declared his position (see Alma 46:12). With the same unrelenting courage, can we in this day thwart the forces of evil now marshaled against the purposes of God? Can we press forward with steadfastness in Christ, having a perfect brightness of hope and a love of God and all men? The words of Nephi are very clear, "Ye [meaning you and me] must press forward" (2 Nephi 31:20). *Press forward* means to keep moving in the right direction with determination and boldness. In my mind I hear my mother's voice sending me off, "Ardeth, come straight home; do not dilly-dally by the wayside." This admonition had greater meaning years later when I read the words of President George Q. Cannon, "You may dally by the wayside; you may fool away your time; you may be idle, indifferent and careless; but you only lose thereby the progress that you ought to make" (*Gospel Truth,* 19).

Can we be a light to the nations in a darkening world? Shall we raise a standard by pressing forward with steadfastness in Christ? This I testify to you: we can—God has made it possible; we will—life has meaning, purpose, and direction; we must—we are women of covenant.

We Can Press Forward

First, we can press forward. Our Savior marked the path and led the way. Through the waters of baptism, we have entered the gate, and, having received the Holy Ghost, we are on the path (see 2 Nephi 31:5). Our Father in Heaven wants us to be happy, supremely happy. He is our Father. The great plan of happiness of which Alma speaks is God's plan for us (see Alma 42:16).

A faithful Bolivian woman who drives her llama herd onto the Altiplano to forage for food each day was visited one evening in her small home by two young missionaries, who taught her about the great plan of happiness, about the mission of the Savior, the doctrine of the Atonement, the resurrection, and the promise of eternal life. Her dark eyes widened, overflowing with tears. Her heart flooded with hope, she whispered to the two young men, "You mean He did that for me?" To her earnest question, the Spirit bore immediate witness, and she again whispered, this time not in question but in reverent awe, "He did that for me." With that testimony burning in her soul, and in ours, as women of God we can press forward with steadfastness in Christ. We can press forward— all the way, every day. He made it possible.

When we determine to take a stand and commit to go the whole way, our whole lives, our Father in Heaven will be with us the whole way, our whole lives. Author C. S. Lewis suggests one analogy: When you go to the dentist to get rid of a toothache, that's all you really want—to be rid of the ache. But the dentist won't stop there. He grinds and grinds until all the decay is removed. Then Lewis adds, "This Helper who will, in the long run, be satisfied with nothing less than absolute perfection, will also be delighted with the first feeble, stumbling effort you make tomorrow to do the simplest duty" (*Mere Christianity,* 171–72).

The straight and narrow path and the rod of iron are not what cause the ache for most of us—we want to be good. It's the rough terrain, with its ups and downs, its trials and tests, that hurts. The pain and heartache, our fears and failures try our faith. At times we may think our Father in Heaven has forgotten us. Looking back we will realize He was with us all along.

> *At the throne I intercede;*
> *For thee ever do I plead.*
> *I have loved thee as thy friend,*
> *With a love that cannot end.*
> *Be obedient, I implore,*
> *Prayerful, watchful, evermore,*
> *And be constant unto me,*
> *That thy Savior I may be.*
>
> ("Reverently and Meekly Now,"
> *Hymns,* no. 185)

Shall we not press forward all the way?

We Will Press Forward

We can and we will press forward. Our Relief Society Declaration reconfirms, "We are beloved spirit daughters of God, and our lives have meaning, purpose, and direction." Once we understand our life's purpose, we begin to plan with a purpose what we are to do and also what we want as a result. That vision of our purpose fills us with life and light. The vision of our eternal possibilities lifts the burden, transforming the weariness of everyday doing to an exhilaration of accomplishing. And our greatest, most valuable accomplishments may well be invisible to the world. As Paul wrote to the Corinthians: "All things are for your sakes. . . . For our light affliction, which is but for a moment, worketh for us a far more exceeding and eternal weight of glory; . . . We look not at the things which are seen, but at the things which are not seen: for the things which are seen are temporal; but the things which are not seen are eternal" (2 Corinthians 4:15, 17–18).

In *The Little Prince,* the fox bids the Prince good-bye, saying: "And now here is my secret, a very simple secret: It is only with the heart that one can see rightly; what is essential is invisible to the eye" (Antoine de Saint

Exupéry, 87). When we press forward with steadfastness in Christ with a perfect brightness of hope, our lives have meaning. We begin not only to look but also to see, not only to talk but also to communicate. Our otherwise routine activities can become an offering on the altar of God. We don't just serve; we nurture. We don't just take our neighbor a loaf of bread; we share the bread of life. We're not just teaching a class; we're changing a life. Our gospel study goes beyond knowing about Him to knowing Him and striving to be filled, as He was, with the love of God. Our lives have meaning and purpose.

With a firm grip on the iron rod but without the vision of the tree of life, we sometimes focus on the blisters on our hands and forget His hands scarred with nail prints. Our vision of what we are working for, what we are living for, and what we want to have happen in our lives elevates us to a higher level of living because it gives meaning to everything we are doing.

When we begin to understand, even in part, the magnitude of the promises of eternal life, then all the doings—the assignments, the calls, the programs, the activities, the dos and the don'ts, the peanut butter and jam smeared on the kitchen table, and yes, even the never-ending laundry—take on a whole new meaning. A burden ceases to be a burden once we see the purpose for it.

Our prayers being more purposeful, they become more answerable. Recently, my niece asked her little four-year-old son, Jake, to give the family prayer, to which he responded in his pure and childlike way, "Mom, I only do food prayers." What is sweet at age four would be truly sad at age forty. And we may still be doing just food prayers at forty unless we have a real purpose for our communication with God. Our Father in Heaven encourages our communication. He says over and over in the scriptures, Ask—ask in faith.

When we pray with purpose, we have power in prayer. President Gordon B. Hinckley told us, "Members can fight evil with prayer." Here are his words: "Believe in getting on your knees every morning and every night and talking to your Father in Heaven concerning the feelings of your hearts and the desires of your minds in righteousness. Believe in prayer. There is nothing like it. When all is said and done there is no power on the earth like the power of prayer" ("President Hinckley Addresses 15,000 in Laie," n. p.).

In answer to our prayers, our Father in Heaven will open doors for us, soften hearts, and heal wounds, spiritual and physical. Put simply, He will just make things better all around, because He wants us to be good and He wants us to be happy. And on occasion, He will direct us to be there in answer to someone else's prayer.

When we press forward in our sometimes stumbling

ways, striving to share the love of God, I believe there are no little things. Corrie ten Boom, in *The Hiding Place,* describes the horrible concentration camp at Ravensbruck. The hot miserable room where she and her sister Betsie were confined was infested with fleas. Corrie came to see it as a blessing because it kept the guards away and allowed her to share her scriptures with other inmates. Hear her words: "Side by side, in the sanctuary of God's fleas, Betsie and I ministered the word of God to all in the room. We sat by deathbeds that became doorways to heaven. We watched women who had lost everything grow rich in hope. . . . We prayed beyond the concrete walls for the healing of Germany, of Europe, of the world—as Mama had once done from the prison of a crippled body" (198–99, 211).

In our lives there will be opposition, trials, and tests of every kind, perhaps not as dramatic as those of Corrie and her sister Betsie, but in God's eyes equally significant, and from His perspective even heroic.

The last Mother's Day before my mom passed away, as I was pushing her in her wheelchair into the chapel, she whispered, half to herself but loud enough for me to hear, "I never liked Mother's Day. It always reminds me of all the things I didn't do as a mother." Wanting to ease her mind, I leaned over and whispered, "Mom, I don't think you did so badly." She smiled.

Mom was never defeated by adversity. When a hailstorm killed Dad's flocks of turkeys, or more than once an early frost destroyed our crops of grain, Mom assured us children that all would be well. She still believed we could have a rich harvest. Dad moved an old granary next to our house, and Mom opened a small grocery store, where she worked her heart out while Dad worked in the fields. They didn't count the number of bushels to the acre, sure evidence of crop failure. They measured their harvest in other ways. Mom didn't teach my two sisters and me to sew and cook and other such things mothers often did, but by her side, in our little country store in Canada, she taught us that our customers from the Blood Indian Reservation, and the Hutterites from the nearby colonies, and the immigrants from across the river were not only our customers but also our friends who deserved our deepest respect and generosity. We needed them, and they needed us. "That's what makes good friends," Mom taught us.

I watched her many times tuck into a bag of groceries a sack of cookies that I noticed she never itemized on the customer's bill. I watched as a child would thoughtfully choose candy from the penny candy counter, have it in the sack and the top twisted, and then at the last minute have a change of mind. Mom never said, "Too late now, dear." It was never too late to help a child feel good. She was never too busy to be concerned for another human being. Would she not qualify as one pressing forward with steadfastness in Christ, having a perfect brightness of hope and a love of God and of all men? There is more than one way to model righteous mothering.

Hailstorms and crop failures will occur in our lives and in our families. Things don't always turn out the way we plan, but don't ever let what you haven't done eclipse all the good you have done and are doing. A hailstorm may destroy the crops, but with faith in God, I solemnly testify it need not prevent a rich harvest.

We Must Press Forward

Finally, in the words of Nephi, "Ye must press forward . . . in Christ" (2 Nephi 31:20). Our testimonies, our commitments, and our covenants may lie deep inside, but until we take a stand and rid our lives of all of the distractions that obscure this treasure, we are not free to press forward in Christ. As long as we remain undecided, uncommitted, and uncovenanted, we remain unanchored, and every wind that blows becomes life threatening. Uncertainty will breed vacillation and confusion. Taking a stand and making a choice secures for us the gift of the Holy Ghost. That gift releases us from crippling doubt, indecision, and confusion. Once we take a stand, we then have access to power and blessings, so much so that we will hardly be able to keep pace with our opportunities. Elder Bruce R. McConkie declared, "There is no price too high, no labor too onerous, no struggle too severe, no sacrifice too great, if out of it all we receive and enjoy the gift of the Holy Ghost" (*A New Witness for the Articles of Faith,* 253).

President Gordon B. Hinckley's words on the eve of the twenty-first century come as a call and a prayer: "May God bless us with a sense of our place in history and having been given that sense, with our need to stand tall and walk with resolution in a manner becoming the Saints of the Most High" ("At the Summit of the Ages," 74).

The Lord, speaking through Joseph Smith, asserts, "There has been a day of calling, but the time has come for a day of choosing" (Doctrine and Covenants 105:35). Eliza R. Snow, in her hymn "The Time Is Far Spent" (*Hymns,* no. 266), echoes those same sentiments:

> *Be fixed in your purpose, for Satan will try you;*
> *The weight of your calling he perfectly knows.*
> *Your path may be thorny, but Jesus is nigh you;*
> *His arm is sufficient, tho demons oppose.*

May God bless us not with borrowed light but with His light, and we shall press forward with vision, with renewed determination, with confidence and commitment.

True to the faith that our parents have cherished,
True to the truth for which martyrs have perished,
To God's command,
Soul, heart, and hand,
Faithful and true we will ever stand.
("True to the Faith," *Hymns,* no. 254)

We can.
We will.
We must.

Chapter 19

a woman's heart

I have come to believe that pondering the significance of a woman's heart can be a very private and sacred experience. It is a woman's heart that reveals her true self as she journeys through the mountain peaks and valleys of this mortal life.

The heart is a symbol of love. The important role of the heart is repeated over and over in the scriptures, "Trust in the Lord with all thine heart" (Proverbs 3:5). "For as he thinketh in his heart, so is he" (Proverbs 23:7). "Have ye received his image in your countenances? Have ye experienced this mighty change in your hearts?" (Alma 5:14). "Open your ears that ye may hear, and your hearts that ye may understand" (Mosiah 2:9). "Cast your mind upon the night that you cried unto me in your heart, that you might know concerning the truth of these things" (Doctrine and Covenants 6:22). "And according to his faith there was a mighty change wrought in his heart" (Alma 5:12).

While there are many changes that become a part of our journey, the only real change of great significance is the change that takes place in our hearts as we better understand what we came to do. We don't need a heart transplant from some generous donor to stay alive spiritually. We just need to value, nurture, and care for the priceless heart that we came with.

Some years ago when I was working with a group of young women I awakened one early morning and went out on the front porch. There I saw a basket of heart-shaped cookies with a note that read: "You are having a heart attack. We love you."

Pasted artistically all across my front door and brick wall were 100 red, pink, and white paper hearts. If this was a heart attack I was feeling, I wished I might provide such an experience for all my neighbors and friends and relatives and even strangers at the grocery store or wherever. The feelings in my heart that morning made my day. I knew someone loved me. We all need to be reminded again and again that we are loved.

Recently, I attended a meeting where the chapel was filled to capacity, including the choir seats. A magnificent choir rendered carefully selected music that penetrated every heart, inviting the Spirit. Everyone was prepared to hear an appropriate message that would warm their hearts. What they had not anticipated was an experience in which they would each take part and discover the power, the strength, the love in the hearts of everyone in attendance.

The plan was presented: each sister in attendance was to team up with another sister. It didn't really matter if they were longtime friends or had been complete strangers until that day. They were asked to stand and face their partners. Adjustments were made until everyone had a partner.

Then the instructions for this experience were given:

> There will be five parts, and each part will last only one or two minutes. Then you will be asked to stop talking and listen for the next step.
>
> *STEP 1.* Say two things about yourself and then two things about your partner, something that might be considered small talk. For example: "I like the color of your blouse." And then your partner takes her turn to say two things about herself and two things about you. Then wait for the next instruction.
>
> *STEP 2.* Remain standing and take a minute to share with each other something that you really value, something that is precious to you, something you are very grateful for. Then wait for the next instruction.

STEP 3. Discuss with each other an idea or a plan you might be willing to work on together with your combined efforts and talents. Then wait for the next instruction.

STEP 4. Share with your partner something that makes your heart heavy, some burden you are carrying (nothing too private), a load maybe few people even know about. Then wait for the next instruction.

STEP 5. As a last step in this brief exchange, share with your partner the feelings of your heart— what you would want to say if this were the last time you would see each other in this earth life. Then be seated.

At the close of this experience, which had lasted not longer than twenty minutes, sisters were spontaneously embracing each other, and many were wiping tears from their eyes, evidence of their hearts being filled to overflowing with love. The chapel was full of sisters who had opened their hearts to each other in a new and special way. Everyone seemed anxious to better understand what this magic was that had opened the floodgate of love.

A few "teams" were invited to come to the front and share their experiences. Some were close family members, others had been complete strangers until that day, and some had been neighbors for a long time but never knew the feelings in each other's hearts before.

The question seemed to be, How did this happen, and could this happen again and again?

A review of the five steps led us to a deeper understanding of the importance of relationships and how we open our hearts to one another.

Step 1 might be referred to as "small talk," like breaking the ice in conversation, where nothing very significant is discussed. Too often this is the usual pattern of our conversations, and we miss opportunities to go deeper.

Step 2 might be referred to as building a relationship of trust. Sharing values invites a bonding experience.

Step 3 provides an opportunity to come together in each other's thoughts, planning together for a common cause.

Step 4 provides an opportunity to know and help carry one another's burdens, as we agreed to in our covenant of baptism (see Mosiah 18:8).

Step 5 changes the casualness of our relationships as we truly open our hearts, and we begin to see each other differently, with hearts filled with love.

It seemed everyone who went through this simple exercise that day had experienced the joy of feeling love and giving love. It would seem that everyone left that afternoon committed to bonding together with shared values and goals.

Those women felt a commitment to help carry one another's burdens and truly be sisters in Zion, doing the work they came to do, to love one another as the Savior loves them.

Letters following the conference were many. One example: "I was raised a Mormon but left the Church after my father died; you gave me great hope that there really are good people in the Church that care about those on the outside."

Such has always been the case. Many of the women from the early days of Church history expressed the desire of their hearts to be a righteous influence and live according to God's will. As we take occasion to study the lives of those women who have gone before us, we are inspired to join this mighty and powerful force whose righteous influence is carried on from one generation to the next.

Consider the righteous desire of Emma Smith, wife of the Prophet Joseph, when he decided to return to Carthage, a fateful decision that would lead to his death. She asked him to give her a blessing. He invited her to write down the blessing she desired and he would sign it upon his return. Emma wrote the blessing, but the Prophet never returned from Carthage. Her words show the greatest desires of her heart. Part of that blessing is as follows: "First of all that I would crave as the richest of heaven's blessings would be wisdom from my Heavenly Father bestowed daily, so that whatever I might do or say, I could not look back at the close of the day with regret, nor neglect the performance of any act that would bring a blessing."

At the close of her writing she shares the feelings of her heart in these tender words: "I desire with all my heart to honor and respect my husband as my head, ever to live in his confidence and by acting in unison with him retain the place which God has given me by his side. . . . I desire to see that I may rejoice with [the daughters of Eve] in the blessings which God has in store for all who are willing to be obedient to his requirements. Finally, I desire that whatever may be my lot through life I may be enabled to acknowledge the hand of God in all things" (copy of blessing in LDS Church Archives).

Emma's heart led her to live a life of love. And there were many, many other such feelings recorded in the tapestry of the lives of great women. My own great-great-grandmother Susan Kent Greene wrote in her journal on February 3, 1875: "I make this covenant to do the very best I can, asking God for wisdom to direct me in that I may walk with Him in all righteousness and truth. I much desire to be pure in heart that I may see God. Help me Lord overcome all evil with good. This covenant with the writings on this page is written with my blood and I have not broken my covenant and trust shall not. Susan K. Greene."

In my own journal, on January 6, 1981, I recorded those thoughts I had read and added my own commitment: "I wish to express the same thoughts and will look forward one day to seeing great-great-grandmother Susan K. Greene, and hope that I can tell her, I have followed her path, kept the faith and all of the covenants with a pure heart. Ardeth Greene Kapp."

The deepest feelings of a woman's heart are captured most impressively in the words to a beautiful song written by Janice Kapp Perry. With her permission, I've included her insightful, inspiring words:

A Woman's Heart

By Janice Kapp Perry

A woman's heart can hold so many dreams
Of lasting love, a home where she is queen
Through all the changing seasons of her life
In sun and rain she keeps her dreams alive
Though rivers of despair may come and go
The pow'r of living water through her flows
And ev'ry guiding truth she has embraced
Will find a place in a woman's heart

A woman's heart can feel so many things
The joys of life that home and fam'ly bring
Compassion swells within her very soul
It is her gift to comfort and console

There is time to weep and a time to mourn
But through her trials a stronger faith is born
From sorrow she will learn that healing grace
Will find a place in a woman's heart

A woman's heart is open to God's love
She shares this gift through ev'ry tender touch
Though heartaches and temptations may arise
Her trusting heart is drawn toward the light
Bestowing tender mercies she is led
To be a gentle shepherd in His stead
And courage that can build another's faith
Finds a place in a woman's heart

A woman's heart can hold so many dreams
She sets her heart on true and sacred things
She will endure because she knows God's grace
Will find a place in a woman's heart.

A righteous woman's heart has no boundaries and is ever changing. May we all feel more compassion, more forgiveness, more gratitude, more patience, more love, more striving within. May we be found doing what we came to do: living a life of love.

Chapter 20

NO GREATER CALL

On my morning walk a few weeks ago, away from my long to-do list and a myriad of things that had seemed to press for my attention, I was impressed by a group of neighbors actively engaged in a major service project. A yard that had been neglected and was now overgrown with weeds and branches had been taken over by a group of helpers. People both young and older were plying shovels, rakes, hoes, and clippers, all working together to restore the natural beauty of the yard. All the debris was piled high on a trailer behind a truck. A clump of bright yellow sunflowers had also been cleaned out and added to the otherwise colorless load to be taken to the dump.

I continued my walk, no longer burdened by my self-imposed pressure of things not yet done, but rather basking in the radiance of the early morning sunlight. I continued my routine walk of about one and a half miles. On my return, the truck and the dedicated laborers were still in place, with their work project nearing completion.

I approached my home, ready, I thought, to begin my own work project, but something about the sunflowers had captured my attention. I had a change of plans. I grabbed a pair of scissors, jumped in the car, and headed back, thinking I would cut enough bright yellow sunflowers to make a bouquet for my kitchen table. There was a message in those flowers that remained bright and beautiful even after they had been cut down.

Upon my return, the truck with its loaded trailer and all the workers were gone. For some reason I still had a feeling that I wanted a bouquet of sunflowers for my kitchen table, even though our own yard, front and back, was filled with flowers of other varieties. I took a short drive to an open field where I thought I remembered seeing some sunflowers. There were plenty and some to spare. With scissors in hand, I cut enough to fill the vase I had in mind to use and returned home. Having arranged the flowers and placed them in the center of the table, I thought I was ready to return to my plans for the day, but my thoughts took me another direction.

I am a Mia Maid teacher (a surprising call at age eighty).

I have nine young women in my class, seven of whom attend regularly. When I had first received this calling, I had taken the opportunity to visit with each young woman and her mother so that I might better understand and appreciate the gifts and talents, the goals and aspirations of the mother and daughter. I hoped in this way to be able to be more supportive and helpful and to show my love.

Phone calls and notes in the mail didn't change the habits of the two girls who were usually missing when we met together as a class. I knew they each had great potential, with gifts and talents to be developed. I hadn't had much previous association with these girls, but I knew with all my heart and soul that they were daughters of our Heavenly Father, who loved them, and I often prayed to know how to reach them.

As I looked at the bouquet on my kitchen table, the importance of the sunflowers opened my mind. Could these sunflowers be an answer to my prayers? I removed two bright yellow flowers from the bouquet and extended my morning walk several blocks to Shannon's door and knocked. There were very loud barking dogs inside but no answer to my continued knocking. I reverently laid one of the sunflowers on the doorstep and walked on to the home of Marty in hopes of making a contact with her. I felt I was on a special errand. I knocked, and her father came to the door.

He quickly explained that his daughter was not at home. I handed the flower to the father and requested that he give it to his daughter and ask her to bring it to class the following morning. He agreed and closed the door.

Returning home, I felt to make a phone call to the home of the noisy dogs. I left a message asking Shannon if she would be willing to come to class and bring the flower I had left for her on the front step, explaining that our Young Women bouquet of flowers would not be complete without hers.

On Sunday morning, I moved the flowers from my kitchen table to the table in our classroom. Just before the class president took her place to call the group to order and quiet their friendly chatter, in walked Shannon carrying a single sunflower and wearing a smile. It was obviously a happy surprise to the class members assembled. And right behind her, almost as if planned, Marty walked in with a bright yellow sunflower in hand. Everyone was smiling and a bit curious. I immediately took the bouquet that had been placed on the table and, holding it toward the girls, explained, "Nothing is complete if any part is missing." Each young woman carefully added her single flower to the bouquet. The powerful lesson for that day was felt by everyone and expressed by some: "It's great when everyone is here."

Each young woman, including the two who brought

their single flowers, also brought her scriptures with her. All of them participated in our class discussion and read from their scriptures, and our hearts were blessed with a greater desire to be in tune with the Spirit. Seeds were planted that day that will be nourished with friendship, love, patience, and continued prayer.

When I see the radiant, beautiful sunflowers that add so much beauty and light wherever they are planted, I am reminded of the divine nature and infinite worth of every daughter and son of God. He has placed in us a sacred trust to reach out to each and every one with love. There is no greater call.

GOD'S LOVE:
PONDER, ASK, ACT

Ponder

The Savior went all the way: through the agony of the Garden
of Gethsemane, where He took upon Himself the sins of
the world, to the cross, where, even in the last moment of
His suffering, He prayed for His crucifiers. He died on the
cross. He gave His life for us. Yes, that is what He did for
you and for me. He gives us a commandment: "That ye
love one another, as I have loved you" (John 15:12).

Ask

Am I doing what I came to do?
Am I getting better at striving to love as Christ loves?
How might I improve my ability to express love?
When do I feel love?
Do I ask and then listen for the promptings of the Spirit?
Do I respond when prompted?

Act

See others as children of God to be loved.
Give a little of your time, which is your life, for others every
day.
Live the gospel of Jesus Christ filled with charity, the pure
love of Christ.
Record at the end of the day, on paper or in your mind, the instances when you felt prompted to become an instrument
in God's hands in reaching out to others with love.
Do what you came to do. Live a life of love.

sources

Andersen, Neil L. "You Know Enough." *Ensign,* November 2008, 13–14.

Ballard, M. Russell. "Women of Righteousness." *Ensign,* April 2002, 66–73.

Blaydes, John, comp. *The Educator's Book of Quotes.* Thousand Oaks, CA: Corwin Press, 2003.

Cannon, George Q. *Gospel Truth.* Classics in Mormon Literature edition. Salt Lake City: Deseret Book, 1987.

Children's Songbook. Salt Lake City: The Church of Jesus Christ of Latter-day Saints, 1989.

Emerson, Ralph Waldo. "Self-Reliance." In *Emerson: Essays and Lectures.* Selected by Joel Porte. New York: Penguin Putnam, 1983, 259–82.

Eyring, Henry B. "O Remember, Remember." *Ensign,* November 2007, 66–69.

Faust, James E. "Self-Esteem: A Great Human Need." *Brigham Young University 1982–83 Fireside and Devotional Speeches.* Provo, UT: University Publications, 1983, 191–95.

Groberg, John H. *The Other Side of Heaven.* Salt Lake City: Deseret Book, 1993.

Hafen, Bruce C. "Women and the Moral Center of Gravity." in *Ye Shall Bear Record of Me: Talks from the 2001 BYU Women's Conference.* Salt Lake City: Deseret Book, 2002, 290–306.

Hinckley, Gordon B. "At the Summit of the Ages." *Ensign,* November 1999, 74.

———. "President Hinckley Addresses 15,000 in Laie." *LDS Church News,* January 29, 2000.

Holland, Jeffrey R. "Remember Lot's Wife." BYU Devotional Address, January

13, 2009. Available at http://www.byub.org/talks/transcripts/devo/2009/1/devo2009113–3403.pdf

Hymns of The Church of Jesus Christ of Latter-day Saints. Salt Lake City: The Church of Jesus Christ of Latter-day Saints, 1985.

Jefferson, Charles Edward. *The Character of Jesus.* New York: Thomas Y. Crowell Company, 1908.

Kimball, Spencer W. *The Miracle of Forgiveness.* Salt Lake City: Bookcraft, 1969.

Lee, Harold B. *The Teachings of Harold B. Lee.* Salt Lake City: Bookcraft, 1996.

Lewis, C. S. *The Four Loves.* New York: Harcourt, 1988.

———. *Mere Christianity.* New York: HarperCollins, 2001.

Lund, Gerald N. *Selected Writings of Gerald N. Lund.* Gospel Scholars Series. Salt Lake City: Deseret Book, 1999.

McConkie, Bruce R. *A New Witness for the Articles of Faith.* Salt Lake City: Deseret Book, 1985.

Merriam-Webster's Collegiate Dictionary. 11th ed. Springfield, MA: Merriam-Webster, Inc., 2005.

Monson, Thomas S. "The Doorway of Love." *Ensign,* October 1996, 2–7.

Oaks, Dallin H. *The Lord's Way.* Salt Lake City: Deseret Book, 1991.

———. "Love and Law." *Ensign,* November 2009, 26–29.

Oaks, Robert C. "Your Divine Heritage." *Ensign,* April 2008, 46–50.

Packer, Boyd K. "Balm of Gilead." *Ensign,* November 1987, 16–18.

———. "Our Moral Environment." *Ensign,* May 1992, 66–68.

———. "Reverence Invites Revelation." *Ensign,* November 1991, 21–22.

———. "Self-Reliance." *Ensign,* August 1975, 85–89.

Perry, L. Tom. "The Importance of the Family." *Ensign,* May 2003, 40–42.

Potok, Chaim. *The Chosen.* New York: Fawcett Crest, 1967.

Pratt, Parley P. *The Essential Parley P. Pratt.* Edited by Peter L. Crawley. Salt Lake City: Signature Books, 1990.

———. *Key to the Science of Theology.* Classics in Mormon Literature edition. Salt Lake City: Deseret Book, 1978.

Remeen, Rachel Naomi. *My Grandfather's Blessings.* New York: Riverhead Books, 2000.

Saint Exupéry, Antoine de. *The Little Prince.* Katherine Woods, trans. New York: Harcourt, Brace & World, 1943.

Swinton, Heidi S. *To the Rescue: The Biography of Thomas S. Monson.* Salt Lake City: Deseret Book, 2010.

Teachings of Presidents of the Church: Joseph Smith. Salt Lake City: The Church of Jesus Christ of Latter-day Saints, 2007.

ten Boom, Corrie. *The Hiding Place.* New York: Bantam Books, 1971.

Uchtdorf, Dieter F. "The Infinite Power of Hope." *Ensign,* November 2008, 21–24.

———. "Of Things That Matter Most." *Ensign,* November 2010, 22.

White, E. B. *Charlotte's Web.* New York: HarperCollins, 1952.